I'M ALMOST OKAY

Navigating the Grief of Parental Loss, Miscarriage, and Divorce

AMANDA LANDES, PSY.D.

For more information, email amanda@imalmostokay.com

ISBN: 979-8-89694-759-2 - Ebook
ISBN: 979-8-89694-760-8 - Paperback
ISBN: 979-8-89694-761-5 - Hardcover

GET YOUR FREE GIFT

Want to take what you've learned from this book wherever you go? I've found readers who download and use The Ten Talking Points of Grief can implement the lessons from the book faster and take the next steps needed to be a supportive caregiver, cope with grief, and manage healthy interpersonal relationships.

You can get a copy by visiting:

www.imalmostokay.com

DEDICATION

This book is dedicated to my father, Alan Landes, who was unexpectedly taken from this plane in 2018 after a four-year battle with glioblastoma multiforme, a rare and aggressive form of brain cancer. While his tragic story is what catapulted me into writing, he was an inspiration to me long before his passing.

Alan was a college tennis coach whose philosophical underpinnings focused on positive approaches to inspiring athletes to succeed. He dreamed of sharing his vision with the world, and we had spoken about writing a book together long before his illness took hold. He was dyslexic and viewed me as a strong writer. He assumed his expertise, coupled with my credibility as a psychologist, would make us an unstoppable team.

We did not get to collaborate as he wished. While I don't know much about the nuances of tennis coaching, I hope that some of his lessons—about staying positive and persevering through hard times—shine through in my story. I wrote this book with a small hologram version of my dad perched on my shoulder, and every word printed is in his honor.

CONTENTS

PREFACE

You may notice that I don't talk much about other people here, and that decision was intentional. Of course, there are other characters in my story, and they all have their own narratives. This one belongs to me. I intend to focus on it without getting caught up in explaining myself or justifying certain actions based on the hypothetical judgments or counterpoints of others.

People may say my version of events isn't correct or that I left out important pieces—maybe they're right. But that's their reality, not mine. Reality is really a series of Venn diagrams, and sometimes the circles overlap more than others. I apologize in advance for what I do and don't say here. If you're offended, it wasn't intentional—and maybe this story isn't for you.

I don't operate with obscure agendas. My hope is simply to put something back into the universe that someone else might find useful in some way. Writing this has been cathartic. I have framed the last decade of my life with these very words in mind. Now, I invite you to proceed with caution, as I have done.

INTRODUCTION

I celebrated my thirtieth birthday lying on a soft beach cabana bed perched atop radiant white sand on the coast of Kauai during the second week of my honeymoon. I smiled as the sun's rays penetrated my skin and the warm ocean breeze kissed my cheeks. *"This is perfect,"* I thought to myself, smiling at my new husband over a bowl of tuna poke from a local deli and a bottle of champagne gifted to us by the concierge of our luxe hotel.

Life did feel perfect. I had just married Sam, my high school sweetheart—the love of my life—and I was only months away from earning my doctoral degree. I assumed I had reached the part of adulthood where all the gears in my world were clicking and whirring in unison. I thought all the kinks had been worked out and there was no chance of a system failure.

It turns out I was wrong. Though I didn't know it as Sam and I sat chatting over the sound of delicate waves lapping the Hawaiian shore, my good fortune was borrowed, not owned—and in three years' time, the collectors would return, demanding what they were owed, plus interest. In three years' time, it would all fall apart.

My miscarriage, coupled with my dad's illness and subsequent death, may not be the worst things that could happen to someone. There are atrocities and personal losses in this world that carry objectively greater weight. I go back and forth between not wanting to minimize or overdramatize my experience of losing so much at once, while also trying to navigate multiple kinds of grief at the same time. I've always felt too self-aware, and it often manifests as an internal battle to decide whether my thoughts and actions are valid. It's a reminder that even after living through the many things I will share with you, I am still a work in progress. I will always be one.

One of the myths I believed in my thirties was that I would suddenly become an adult with all the answers and perspective my predecessors had—as if being a fully functioning person were some unexclusive club, and we all ultimately made it past the bouncer.

Since then, I've learned that not everyone makes it past the bouncer and that real adulthood lies in continually trying to find new ways to make it inside—while appreciating all the characters we meet in line.

I digress. Prepare yourself—because I often do. Life rarely unfolds as neatly as I'd like. Part of telling the story involves determining how far I've come—and filling in the gaps. The gaps are growth, and they are exceptionally important, even if they lead down meandering paths that are tough to navigate back from.

In my experience, life—and stories—seldom unfurl in straight lines. Life is more like a winding road, and that's part of the reason the back-and-forth matters. I'm sure someone will correct me if I'm wrong. So, though my story may not be the worst thing that could happen to someone, it is the worst thing that happened to me—and it changed me in indelible ways. Some for the better. Some not.

Once, in the midst of living this story, a person I loved and trusted told me, *"You can't be eternally ruined by something."* I believe that is true. Being ruined is a choice, in my opinion. However, the things that happen to us still become part of who we are. We are continually changed by the moment-to-moment circumstances we encounter, to some degree.

Like a sea cliff lapped by decades of waves, I am different than I was yesterday or earlier this morning. Generally, people don't change dramatically from one minute to the next, but our experiences are cumulative. Each choice is a grain of sand that builds up over time and can either bury us or shape us. So, I was not ruined by my negative life events, but those events have altered and continue to inform how I view the world.

Before everything unraveled, my perspective was straightforward. I internalized the messages I received from my family, from school, and from organized religion. I saw life as a formula: success equaled my effort over time. Like those high school logic problems—*if P, then Q*—it all seemed fairly controllable. Keep your head down, do what you're supposed to do, and it will all be okay.

My grandmother told me that I was the only child she knew who came directly home from school and started my homework without being asked. Rules, expectations, and structure gave me autonomy and control. I was hungry for that sense of order from a young age. Even when I hated school, even when the world around me was a tornado, I sat at a desk studying for a vocabulary test.

Sure, I had difficult experiences before my mid-thirties—death, discord, and other stories better suited for another time. But they felt external to me—the result of someone else's miscalculation. My formula had taken me pretty far: a doctorate, a good job, a supportive group of friends and family, and financial stability. I generally did not think bad things could happen to me—not because I thought I was better than hard times or because I was grandiose about what I was, but simply because it never crossed my mind as a possibility.

Much in the same way that, as a child, I assumed clean houses and nice things were for other people, the truly horrific seemed for other people too. Everything changed with a phone call—the first of many dominoes made of sewage that would fall over the next several years and eviscerate my life.

ONE

What are you doing?

"What are you doing?" My dad's calm, breezy voice floated through the Bluetooth headset I wore while driving. It was his typical phone greeting, and I hated it. No *hello*, no *hi, it's Dad, how are you?*, no *good morning.* Just a question that seemed intrusive and inappropriately placed. My dad's "what are you doing?" always made me feel judged, as if, on some deeper philosophical level, he was questioning more than what I was doing at the moment he called me. It felt like my life choices were up for discussion. Maybe they should have been. Maybe some part of me knew I deserved the judgment.

Either way, it was his thing until he started to get sick, and when it was gone, I noticed its absence—like one realizes when your elderly great aunt, who unintentionally spits in the food when she talks and gives wet kisses, is no longer at Thanksgiving dinner. I am aware that the reference is oddly specific.

Sometimes I answered the phone already upset—snippy, as my dad would unhelpfully identify it. I would counter "What are you doing?" with an edginess that I made no effort to tamp down. Sometimes he ignored my tone. Sometimes he asked me if I was okay, which was typically enough to ease my irritation, and I would tell him I was fine. He would readily offer up what he was doing. He didn't see why it was a big deal. Often, as was the case on the day of the phone call in question, I was not snippy. I told him I was driving, and the substance of our conversation began.

He nonchalantly mentioned his memory—how he noticed he was having some trouble recalling common words that he used all the time, like *broccoli*. He'd know the word he was trying to say but could not access it—as if it were stuck behind a locked bank vault in his brain and he did not know the passcode to set it free. He'd describe the item instead, hoping the person he was talking to could guess it. I didn't pay much attention to it. I probably just said *"okay"* and then we went on to talk about something else.

I assumed my athletically built dad, who had spent his whole life taking pride in his health and eating habits, was looking for some justification to stop taking the cholesterol medication that he was shocked to need in the first place. He had read something about cholesterol medication depleting some of the good fats in our brains and that their absence was correlated with memory deficits. Problem and solution. It was neat. I liked it. He eventually spoke to his primary care physician about his memory, and his doctor stopped the medication without question. My dad was happy. He remarked that his memory was getting better about a week later. Case closed.

Speaking to my dad during my hour-long commute home from my job at a school on Long Island had become a ritual for us. My dad had recently moved from Long Island to Manhattan and commuted to work in Queens. Though we checked in every day about traffic and work, there were hints in his tone—small pauses when he couldn't recall a word—that I ignored. They should have been the warning signs. At the time, I assumed he was tired or distracted when his voice sounded distant or when he repeated a story he had already told me the day before. I never thought my dad could be anything other than okay. I never assumed he was invincible, but I certainly did not see him as vulnerable.

By the time my dad stopped his cholesterol medication, I was preparing to leave my life in urban, industrial Queens to move about an hour north of the city for a job that would be the start of my career as a forensic psychologist. While I was excited about my new opportunities, I couldn't shake the feeling that they would contribute to me drifting further from my dad. We would have fewer casual chances to see one another and lose the opportunity to commiserate over shared commuter traffic. I was optimistic that we would figure it out and remain close—that the phone calls would continue and that they would be enough.

Everything felt important and exciting. Life was making sense. I was in control. I was figuring it all out. My decisions were setting me on a clear path to happiness and functional adulthood. I was confident in my choices and had empathy, maybe even pity, for people I viewed as less put together than myself.

The thirty-two-year-old version of me would not have believed you if you had told her that in less than a year's time, everything would feel completely different—that the pillars of my life, which I had meticulously built and cautiously stood upon, would be knocked out from beneath me. Though they would be rebuilt, there would be a lot of casualties in the construction, and they would never look the same.

Psychologists talk about how the moments preceding significant life events get embedded in our brains, encoded in ways that are triggered by our senses. I can tell you what the sky looked like the morning of September 11th, how the color was a blue that mimicked the clearest Caribbean ocean, dotted with sparse white clouds like distant islands. I can tell you what the air smelled like later that day and in the weeks after—how the smoke that wafted a mile up to my Union Square dorm was a mix of fire, debris, and corpses, and how that smell cloaked my friends and me in sadness for months after, particularly when the wind picked up.

Similarly, I know a lot about the day my dad helped me move upstate, as it was the last time things felt as they had always felt between us. I hesitate to say *normal*, because normal isn't a solid state. After the move, our existence devolved into a new normal— one that was predictable but not at all comforting. One that always felt like searching for home rather than finding it.

Moving day was one of those oppressive summer mornings that drained the city—when heat emanates a couple of inches up from the sidewalk, licking your ankles, and the concrete stinks of dog urine. Moving was hectic, even though some friends came over to help. But even in the middle of all that chaos, I was excited to see my dad—to be able to depend on him one last time before geography forced my hand at increased independence. Looking forward to my new life while simultaneously mourning what I was sacrificing for it filled me with ambivalence. I was happy to be carving my own path, but I also wondered who would come help me if I got a flat tire or meet me for lunch on a whim, since my dad wouldn't be able to.

Sam and I had a tight circle of loyal and strong friends who were there to help us and were without much to do until the boxes were taped shut and the movers showed up. The five guys stayed outside on the nearly deserted two-lane street that butted up to my apartment building, casually tossing a football across the road to one another when my father arrived. They knew him from our wedding and various other social gatherings over the years and greeted him with the same affable goofiness that they reserved for most people with whom they felt comfortable.

"Hey, Mr. L!" someone yelled.

"Yo, that's Amanda's dad. From the wedding," another proclaimed.

I watched from the window as my dad offered elevator courtesy greetings as he passed them and entered the white marble lobby of my building.

Nothing makes a generally serious man more serious than being thrust into youthful tomfoolery. "That's some crew out there," he mused with a smirk when he got upstairs. His smile dripped into a scowl as he scanned my living room and saw the unfinished packing before him. "What are you doing?" he asked me. And before I could answer, "Let's go." His voice sounded as if someone were pinching his nose shut as he directed me to hurry up.

He told me he had a cold. I didn't often hear my dad sick, and the sound was disarming. He was on the short list of responsible grown-up adults that I knew, and people in that category seemed as if they should be immune to the types of illnesses that take down the masses of less reasonable humans ambling about the earth. He insisted he was fine, but I could tell something was off. His usual certainty, the strength in his voice, had been replaced by an unfamiliar weariness.

I asked him if he was up to helping, and he assured me that he was. I can see him there, leaning against an un-taped box in front of a nearly floor-to-ceiling window that framed the East River and Midtown Manhattan, in cargo shorts that were too long for a man of his age—cargo shorts he only started wearing after he married a much younger woman, a dusty blue long-sleeved Queens College Men's Tennis shirt, a U.S. Open Tennis hat, and Oakley sunglasses strung around his neck by something that looked like a soft neon yellow straw. He stared out the window as I scurried around, trying not to feel like a burden.

My dad and I were tasked with taking his car upstate to my new rental house to meet the movers when they arrived. Sam was coming in a second car with our cat, our boxer, and whatever other miscellaneous items hadn't made it into the moving truck. My dad was adamant that no animals accompany us in his car. He had a general dislike of cats, and while he tolerated dogs, he drew a line at commuting with either one of them. It took about an hour and a half to get to my new rental house in the woods, and we chatted in the car about our lives and the ways in which marriages and children can shape them—advice mixed with reflections on his experiences. It felt good to spend time alone with him in person and not just in separate cars going in opposite directions, talking about the traffic.

****

My dad and I struggled to find much in-person time in the year prior to my move; our lives were propelling forward on diverging paths, and the natural momentum created some distance. Before branching away from one another, I was getting my doctorate at a school close to his suburban home and often stopped by for dinner after class with him, my stepmother Camilla, and my much younger sister Lia, who was a toddler at the time. My dad developed a very limited cooking repertoire after marrying Camilla, which consisted of pasta with meat sauce, and tacos—both cooked with a ground soy product that yearned to be beef. He was proud of his culinary offerings and was eager for me to partake.

"See?" he'd question, with the wonder and excitement of a child who saw his first nighttime sky full of stars. "It tastes just like the real thing." The meat substitute did not, in fact, taste like the real thing. I endured the dinners because of what they represented. We were doing regular family things—cooking, laughing, sitting together at a table—and the value of the time spent outweighed whatever it was that he served.

In addition to his culinary offerings, he got me a part-time job at Queens College working nights to manage the tennis courts. The job mainly consisted of corralling difficult and entitled seniors and cleaning up the abandoned water bottles, crumpled chip bags, and clear plastic tubes with metal pop ring tops that housed new tennis balls. Sometimes, I had to muster up authoritative energy to kick players off the courts when they had gone past their time and were unwilling to relent. Annoyed, they would yell, "Don't you know who I am?" Most often, I did not know who they were and did not care either—truly relevant people with managed egos never have to ask that question.

There was a stark contrast between my daytime hours spent in academia, pontificating about psychological theories, and my nighttime hours getting scolded by elderly pseudo-elites—that was probably my dad's way of keeping me grounded. I did not love learning that lesson in the moment, but the job offered me plenty of downtime for schoolwork in my small, windowless office— the only consistent sounds being massive vent fans circulating air through the white, egg-shaped tennis bubble that housed the courts, occasionally pierced by sneakers squeaking across the green asphalt below. Plus, I was allowed to use the college gym, where my dad and I regularly met to work out together. Some nights we'd talk when our routes crossed at the end of his workday and the beginning of my shift. Some nights, he'd bring me a sports drink and make sure I had dinner.

Queens College had been a centralizing point in my lifeline. My dad began coaching the men's tennis team the year I was born, so I spent a lot of hours there as a young child. I learned how to walk on the paths outside the tennis courts. The concrete walkways outlining academic buildings guided me as I got acquainted with riding a bike. My dad's tennis teams became our extended family, and it was not uncommon to find his players at our holiday dinners when they were unable to travel home to theirs. Family vacations were frequently interwoven with interstate tennis matches, and I often found myself at Disney World or at a pool, being tossed around by a dozen big brothers.

I spent the summer after my freshman year of college at the Queens College day camp pool, working as a lifeguard assistant; I did not become a lifeguard, as I had been too afraid to swim down to the deep end of the pool to pick up a brick from the bottom. But my dad and the community he built within the college athletics department found me a job. I took tennis and swim lessons at Queens College and frequently met my dad for lunch at whatever chain restaurant in the student center struck his fancy—he'd get very enthusiastic about a good lunch special. There were more than a handful of conversations about new places opening and which restaurant had the best deal. He would walk around the dining hall like a seasoned tour guide, pointing: "Here you get soup with lunch, but there you get soup and soda." He was passionate about the whole meal-sharing experience, as if he were on some archaeological dig comparing newly discovered burial grounds.

I spent less time at the college once grad school was done. I got my first adult job, and my dad moved into Manhattan. The frequency of the time my dad and I spent alone decreased and was replaced by dinners and outings with partners and family while I focused on my own microcosm of boyfriends, nights out with friends, and work.

****

I didn't see my dad the winter after my move. Neither of us was big on the cold weather, and living upstate made it harder to socialize because of all the driving or train riding that a day out entailed. We talked a lot, and that was almost enough. I remember being excited when FaceTime became a thing. I told him, "Now we can talk and see each other, Dad," and his reply was, "That's okay. I don't need to see you."

"Okay," I answered with raised eyebrows, letting his comment roll off. I didn't take it personally. He had this inoffensive bluntness to him that I had grown to appreciate. As a child and teenager, I didn't find it quite as charming, which is one of the reasons our relationship didn't get to where it ended up until I was close to graduating high school.

My dad wasn't shy about his preference for adult children over younger ones—it was easier for him to relate to them and to be understood. There was less of the game-playing and silliness that made him uncomfortable. He worked a lot when I was small, and I spent most weekends with my mom or my friends. He was an elementary school computer teacher by day and a tennis coach the rest of the time. He retired early from his day job when I started high school, which left him tasked with driving me to and from school, an arrangement neither of us loved, particularly in the mornings.

He did not like to get up early, so my 7:20 a.m. school start time was an affront to his circadian rhythm. The norm was for him to emerge from bed in sweatpants and a wrinkled T-shirt that smelled like sleep, and wordlessly maneuver to the car with unbrushed teeth. I hated it. It was all so embarrassing. I spent most drives shoulder to shoulder with the passenger side door of the car in an attempt to put as much space between my dad and me as possible, similar to how one inches away from a neighbor on a crowded subway who neglected to apply deodorant before beginning their morning commute. Despite living out of district and about twenty minutes away from my high school, I worried that somehow someone would see me with him and that there would be social consequences.

We typically drove in silence and listened to sports talk radio, which I also hated. Those men had such an angry and abrasive cadence to their banter, and it baffled me that a non-morning person such as my father found their squawks not only tolerable but optimal. I felt suffocated in a car full of morning breath and aggressive sports commentary as I sank low in my seat and stared out the window at the pastel-colored early morning world. I felt sorry for myself in the way that only teenagers, with their sliver of understanding of life, can.

We said our goodbyes around the block from school, partially so my dad could avoid traffic and partially so I wouldn't be judged for being driven to school by my dad, which felt life-ending when I was fifteen. I walked the rest of the way, headphones in, erasing the discomfort of the drive with some mixtape that rotated through Nirvana, R.E.M., or a myriad of Riot Grrrl bands playing from the cassette player safety-pinned into the pocket of my zip-up hoodie sweatshirt that I donned, no matter the temperature. For reasons my adult brain can no longer understand, it felt supremely uncool to emerge from a car, as if all the kids who were comfortable—the ones who knew and liked themselves—somehow spontaneously appeared in front of the school, with their outfits, their friends, and all of their shit together. I needed that half-block walk to get into my cool teenager costume for the day.

Our after school drives home were different. By then, my dad had time to reanimate, to turn back into the clean-clothed, brushed-teeth person I was comfortable with. He met me around the block from school, leaning up against his white Chrysler Sebring convertible with the soft black top, a cup of soup or a sandwich in hand. He liked a deli he passed somewhere along the way, and he'd talk about the specials with a wide-eyed smile, proud to have found us a mutually enjoyable topic. He taught me about the wonders of combining turkey, provolone, and Russian dressing on a hard roll.

On warm afternoons, we drove to the Bayside marina and sat on the pier, eating our lunches and watching the birds and boats bob in the brown, opaque bay water. On rarer occasions, we drove a half-hour out to Jones Beach, walked the boardwalk, and got ice cream. The beach, with its ocean sounds and smells, was a constant point of connection for my dad and me. I could see the tension melt away from the corners of his eyes and mouth as he stared out over the horizon, his retinas tracing the flight paths of cawing gulls as they floated across the ocean sky.

On an early spring afternoon of my senior year in high school, my dad told me he wanted to show me where he had lived as a kid, and we drove to his old neighborhood. My dad grew up in Brooklyn, and he seldom spoke of his youth for all the reasons emotionally guarded adults with difficult upbringings choose not to share, so the drive to Brooklyn was a big deal. From what I know, he did not have a good childhood. His parents, my grandparents, had their struggles. My parents used to refer to my grandmother as *cuckoo* or *wacky*, and as a child, I knew that meant she was in and out of hospitals and received shock treatments. When she was well, she was a sweet old lady who brought me adult-sized slip-on fuzzy slippers when she visited, and my mom would cut the heels off so I could wear them without falling.

As an adult psychologist, I assume that my grandmother had some sort of cycling mood disorder, possibly with psychotic features. Growing up with my grandmother as a mother had a larger impact on my dad than just giggling about oversized shoes. He was quiet about his past, and there was a sadness to him on the rare occasions when it did come up. At some point in his youth, she told him that he had been a failed abortion, a whispered anecdote shared with me by my mother when I was too young to hear it. My dad never told me that story. I certainly never asked. He did not speak freely about his mom, and the time we spent with her felt more like an obligation than a joy.

"Why do you want to go here today?" I asked.

"Because I just do," he said.

I wondered what was going through his head as the car bumped over Brooklyn highway potholes, which felt as if we were traversing miniature mountain ranges. Not yet insightful enough to know what questions to ask about his impromptu road trip, and not yet confident enough to ask them, I was a quiet observer.

I saw the urban street where he was raised. I saw his old house, narrow and white, sandwiched between two identical houses and bordered by a small rectangular strip of grass, just beginning to turn from brown to green as warmer temperatures settled in. He didn't tell me what he wanted me to see or what he was looking for, but it felt important. I was pretty sure nobody else in our family had seen his childhood home—*not my mother, not my older sister Gwenn.* We sat silently next to one another in the car, staring through his windshield at what had become someone else's real estate, somebody else's unknown story. It was the one and only time he shared that part of himself with me, and I never got the context. I wonder if he felt old ghosts rise up there in the same way that I do when I return to places where he and I had been.

I knew fewer than a handful of stories about my dad's early life. One was that he lived atop a big hill, and in high school, he fell in love with a girl who lived at the bottom of the hill. The hill was ultimately the demise of their relationship, as he did not want to descend, and she did not want to ascend, so they eventually stopped seeing each other. He thought regretfully of stupid teenage decisions, particularly during times when he and my mother were fighting, or when his first marriage was on his mind.

On our drive, he pointed out the window at the hill and said, "This is the hill." It was pretty steep and long. As someone who had not yet experienced true emotional connection, I could understand how a long, hard walk didn't feel worth it. He showed me her house and noted, with an adult's eye, that the distance seemed much smaller than he remembered it as a teenager.

Another anecdote my father shared about his youth was that he used to get beat up by the Italian kids for being Jewish. "You killed Jesus," they'd chant as they shoved him after school. He was by no means religious, referring to himself as agnostic, but he was protective of his cultural origins because of how he had to fight for them when he was young. On rarer occasions, he mentioned that his sister, who was much older than him, left their household when she turned eighteen and how he never forgave her for abandoning him. I imagine a lot happened between the girl down the hill, taking punches for a religion he did not feel connected to, and losing one's sister, but that's all anyone ever got from him. I sometimes think about all the other stories that must have rattled in his brain and felt too unsafe to discuss.

****

For years, I've tried to look at situations objectively, categorizing them as "good" or "not good." I can beat my chest and say this book is about the worst things that happened to me because I can do a comparative analysis with what, prior to this experience, I had identified as the worst thing to happen to me—and assess that the events surrounding my dad's death felt worse and lasted longer. So much longer.

My previous worst thing happened in my twenties and also involved my dad. It was a single snowy day in February 2000—the day of my grandmother's funeral. My dad's mother had spent the later part of her life in a state hospital due to medical problems that were preceded by the psychiatric ones. The hospital was a huge, scary place that surely served as the basis for any hospital ever depicted in a horror movie or television show. The worn brick facility loomed above the smaller, dilapidated buildings that dotted Roosevelt Island in the 1980s and was crowned by the Roosevelt Island Tram of *King Kong* fame.

As a child, I visited my grandmother in this ominous place on sporadic Sundays with my parents. There was a large lawn surrounding the entryway, and on warm mornings, the open space was full of limp amputees propped up in wheelchairs, driven by stone-faced attendants who looked through passersby. Orange-and-white-striped cats with cropped tails—Manx cats, as they are called—rubbed lazily against the concrete benches that framed the sidewalk leading up to the hospital's entrance. I looked at the cats with fear, assuming their tails had been cut off, and whispered to my mom, "Even the cats are missing parts here."

Patients, visitors, staff—nobody enjoyed being at that hospital. Maybe the cats liked it. Everyone looked tense and uncomfortable, like they were carrying invisible, thousand-pound packs of explosives on their shoulders. I remember sitting beside my grandmother's bed on a high, cream-colored radiator with peeling paint, coloring in activity books while the adults made small talk, and how my mom wouldn't let me drink from the water fountains.

I woke up one night in the throes of a nightmare, crying about the place. After that, my dad decided to discontinue my visits. His rule remained in place late into my teenage years, long after I had started to gain some understanding of the situation and thought it might be nice for my dad to have support. I offered to join him on the hospital trips, but he refused, going by himself and returning home somber.

One evening, toward the end of my grandmother's life, my dad received a call from hospital staff, informing him that my grandmother's roommate had shuffled over to her bed with a rolled-up piece of newspaper and a lighter in hand, intending to set my bedridden grandmother on fire. The worker assured my dad that she was unharmed and was being moved to another room. "I get it," my dad chuckled before thanking them and hanging up the phone. He truly understood how someone could feel compelled to torch his mother, which felt hilarious and tragic at the same time.

By the time my grandmother died, I was far removed from my feelings about her or the hospital. I had just started my second semester of college and was consumed with all the things that occupy a young adult living on her own. The funeral was a planned graveside service at a cemetery in New Jersey, to be attended by immediate family: my parents, Gwenn, and my aunt and uncle, whom I had also not seen in years due to turbulence that I did not—and still do not—understand.

It was snowing the morning of the funeral—maybe it was a blizzard—and my father called me as I was awkwardly deciphering what to wear to a graveside service in the snow. He sounded emotionally distant, which was not uncommon. "What do you want to do today? Your sister isn't coming. She said there's too much snow."

He affirmed that nothing was being canceled, and I told him I wanted to go as long as he was going. He and my mother picked me up from my Greenwich Village dorm, and we drove slowly to the white, blurry suburbs. My dad was quiet most of the way, his eyes fixed on the black roads that had turned gray from slush. By the time we got there, the cemetery was a sprawling map of headstones peeking out from fluffy white blankets. We greeted my aunt and uncle formally by the grave. The atmosphere was heavy, distant—uncomfortable in the way silence can be when it's soaked in years of unresolved conflict.

My father and his sister had not seen one another in years, only speaking occasionally to share information about their mother. It was cold. I don't remember much about the service—just the cold and my aunt's black leather gloves, cradling a small box. She explained that the box contained the remnants of her son, my cousin, who had been murdered in Mexico about a year earlier. She talked about how hard it was to get his remains back from Mexico and how they initially sent another person's remains—something she didn't realize until after a DNA test.

The box was all she had left of someone who had always seemed to be the happiest of the bunch—the older cousin who used to toss me around and laugh with me during family gatherings, back when those still happened. My aunt wanted to bury the remains with my grandmother, which came as a surprise. I felt my stomach shrivel and ache low in my body. She wailed as she placed the box on top of my grandmother's coffin, wanting them to rest together. Snow-speckled dirt slowly covered their mingled remains while my uncle held my aunt, his body a shield for her grief. I felt numb and sad and confused and overwhelmed. Typical funeral stuff—but amplified by circumstance.

Afterward, we had a brief, tense exchange with my aunt and uncle that did not go well. My dad was not one for yelling or rehashing old issues, so I didn't hear what he said. But it must have been upsetting enough for my aunt and uncle to address me. My uncle turned to me from up ahead, raising his voice over my aunt's cries: "Amanda, your dad is a terrible person, but we will always love you." I am crying now as I write about this. It was such a hugely pivotal moment for me. The day felt like a discarded soap opera script—death, murder, conspiracies about human remains, a snowstorm. It was all too much. I walked to the car with my father in silence, and my mom walked with my aunt and uncle, seemingly unaffected by the events that had just transpired.

I remember feeling so badly for my dad. He looked vulnerable and alone, as if the confrontation had broken some deeply hidden part of him he didn't realize was still there. His posture deflated, and he looked at the ground. I didn't understand what had happened, but I took his side—and that was probably the moment our relationship began to shift, when I started seeing him as more than just a father. I wanted to protect him and know him. That funeral day ultimately opened the door to some very hard conversations that helped shape our dynamic and form our bond.

Before all the epiphanies and closeness, we drove back to Manhattan and went to Gwenn's apartment for bagels. The snow had mostly stopped by then, and we had a brunch that seemed normal—if not preceded by the events of the morning. My family chatted about inconsequential things. In silence, I thought about everything that had happened, trying to decipher how I felt about it all. There in Gwenn's East Side apartment, sitting on her parquet amber wood floors, I confirmed that day was objectively the worst day of my life.

"Why are you so quiet, Mand?" asked Gwenn. Maybe that's when I became cynical.

With what now feels like a marathon's worth of time behind me, I sometimes long for the days when grief could be contained— when a single terrible day could be bookended by wintry car rides and bagels. The story of my dad getting sick and dying was not that; it became my boundaryless existence, and it moved like an amoeba for more than three years—one endless sorrow absorbing smaller, discrete heartbreaks. I miss my dad. I miss who he was and the relationship we had. I should probably get on with it, so maybe you can see why.

TWO

What funerals give us and parties take

A fternoon drives and my grandmother's ridiculous funeral transformed my dad from a two-dimensional father into a three-dimensional human. It took me twenty years to see him. With an adult's eye, I look back and feel badly that we did not become acquainted sooner. Although I think about all the potential moments we missed, the connections that never formed, I try not to get stuck in that place. I do not take responsibility for all the things that were beyond my control as a child, nor do I blame the younger version of myself for not being closer to my father. I recognize that much of our childhood relationships get muddled by outside influences—by the unspoken hurts and complicated agendas of the adults around us. We accept what we are told because adults know better; they are the authority. We don't expect to be lied to, manipulated, or misinformed, but sometimes that happens, and the only thing to do is fix it when we realize that we can.

Growing up, there were people in my life who painted incomplete pictures of my dad—oversimplified or inaccurate explanations of him. When I was young, there were some things that made me angry about my dad and kept me from feeling close to him. I internalized one-sided information about why he worked so many weekends or why he was withdrawn when he was home. He never shared his position, and I assumed it was because he did not have one. I later learned that he was keeping quiet because he felt it was the right thing to do. He did not want me in the middle of adult arguments and did not want to be the cause of my inner turmoil. He was protecting me the best way he knew how, even though he knew it was at his own expense. I chose to have a bond with my dad as soon as I was old enough to see its value. I realized I wanted him in my corner. While I remember what feels like the injustices of childhood, I chose to focus on how grateful I am to have had him as a meaningful player in my life for as long as I did.

My dad waited patiently for me to gain my own perspectives, to think independently. Once I did, we became exceptionally close. At times, I wondered if we were too close. He confided in me when he was thinking of leaving my mother and when he was hurt by the flaky twenty-something he started dating shortly thereafter. He shared secrets from his first marriage and his sometimes-controversial opinions about our other relatives.

I heard his stories about tennis conferences with other college coaches and how he was nicknamed "Landshark," which made me wince with awkwardness and made him proud. I heard the story—thankfully not all the details—of how he went to his first strip club with his college coach friends and how he was not impressed. It was not my favorite story. I tolerated hearing about it because he seemed happy to be included in activities with men he could relate to, even if it meant going to the occasional strip club in some random travel district in North Carolina.

I was comfortable listening to my dad and helping him through his struggles, and he did the same for me. My dad was the first person I'd call crying when I got dumped or cheated on. I sought out his calm, rational perspective during life's emotionally crushing moments. He didn't always know what to say, but he knew what not to say. My dad never asked me the kinds of questions that stem more from self-interest than support. He didn't give cliché advice. Most of the time, he said very little as he put his arm around my shoulders and made reservations to take me out to dinner. I got a "What are you doing?" every so often as I wept over relationships that I didn't realize were no longer worth my time.

****

My dad and I talked regularly the winter after I moved. I spoke to him about my new job and what it was like working with "the mentally ill criminals," as he called them. I told him about the snow—there was so much snow—and how the nights were cloaked in the kind of darkness and silence that made it hard to sleep. He occasionally brought up his memory problems and how they were getting better, which I doubted. I began to notice that he paused more in conversation, searching for words that escaped him. It was subtle, but it was there. I began to worry about early-onset dementia.

The next time I saw him was in March. Sam and I had spent all winter broke, as he had been out of work and we were trying to sell our high-rise condo in Queens. Our mortgage, our rent, and our life expenses all depended on my paycheck, and there was no wiggle room for the kinds of outings or activities that I typically relied on to distract myself from hard times. We finally closed on our condo on St. Patrick's Day in a Manhattan lawyer's office. After what felt like endless hours of signing papers, we met my dad for lunch at Rosa Mexicana, a Mexican restaurant he liked in Midtown.

I was full of hope about how much easier life was about to get. A huge financial problem was solved. I smiled for the first time in months as we walked toward the restaurant down a gray city sidewalk, guarded by skyscrapers standing shoulder to shoulder. Everything would be simple again. Everything would return to feeling right.

Someone caught my eye as we advanced toward our destination. It felt strange to see a man standing alone, dressed in gray sweatpants and a leather jacket, leaning against the painted red brick of the moderate upscale restaurant where we were headed—a restaurant likely filled with professionals dining over power lunches and expensed meetings. I felt the nerves in my arms tingle as we approached. I pondered hypothetical options to stay safe if we had to pass by him to gain entry to our destination. This disheveled man, with unbrushed hair, a later-than-five-o'clock shadow, and pale skin, triggered within me the same hypervigilance I experienced when I encountered a stranger late at night while alone on a subway platform.

His facial features came into focus as we neared the door. The corners of his mouth turned upward into a faint smile, and as we locked eyes, I realized this man—who appeared as if he had shrunk in his clothes while they remained the same size—was my father. Questions swirled through my brain like a river current after a rainstorm: What happened to my dad? How can he look completely different from the man who had helped me move from the city to the country seven months prior?

I assume lots of people have those moments when they realize their parents are getting old and are less adept at being adults than they were in a previously familiar way. My mother is still alive, and I had a similar insight with her, but it was not instantaneous and was less unexpected. When I was a child, my mother was like a live electrical wire someone had cut without turning off the power—energetic, fiery, and up for anything. We spent our weekends up early and busy, and that momentum continued throughout my twenties. We shopped, took day trips to Great Adventure, and visited small "cutesy towns," as she called them. The cool kid costume I donned in high school did not deter her from making me do things. She got really into Bon Jovi, and I must have seen them in concert with her half a dozen times during that phase. There was also a Broadway show phase that I could not escape.

There was one winter break when she was in her fifties that she drove us home from Florida to beat a snowstorm so I could spend New Year's Eve in my Chinatown NYU dorm with my college boyfriend. She drove nonstop—eighteen hours straight. We had agreed to share the driving at the beginning of the trip, but she wouldn't let me help. She just drove and drove. Over the last ten years, she gradually got slower. She needed to rest more when we embarked on day-long trips to the outlet malls. She got tired quicker and had more trouble driving at night. Her knees hurt, and she fell more. It has been a tough transition, but the slow progression helps it make sense. It's easier because she is not encumbered by the cognitive issues that can turn our loved ones into strangers. With my dad, it was like he got trapped under an avalanche of old man skin cells: one minute he seemed fine; the next, he was not.

Seeing my dad look old on a cold, gray Manhattan afternoon was shocking, and I wasn't sure what to make of it. When I got closer, he seemed less homeless and more like my dad, but a time-lapsed version. I can't recall what we spoke about at lunch, other than the apartment closing. I was quieter than usual, studying his movements and mannerisms to try to draw some reasonable conclusions regarding his changed appearance. I couldn't pinpoint anything, other than that he seemed tired. I made a mental note to call Gwenn about what I had experienced. We finished lunch, said our goodbyes, and I was transported back to my upstate life via Metro-North.

In the subsequent months, my dad insisted that his memory was better without cholesterol medication, and I began to wonder who he was trying to convince. There were more times when he couldn't think of a word and would have to describe it, eliciting suggestions from me to figure out what he was trying to say—conversational charades that nobody ever really won. He started making lists of the words that particularly plagued him, as if he were doing his own detective work on his case. He studied the lists and boasted about times when he remembered a word that had been difficult for him, only to find it replaced by a new lost word. Once, when he got very sick and Camilla had his phone, she found an office-directory-length list of words he had noted. There were hundreds of them. We never knew how hard he was trying to compensate for whatever was happening to him.

Things were very different when I saw my dad again. We were in Florida for my niece's Bat Mitzvah. For those of you who didn't have to endure years of Hebrew school, a Bat Mitzvah is a traditional Jewish ceremony signaling a child's transition to adulthood. There are prayers, Hebrew readings, and singing, often followed by a party to celebrate. Think of it like a cross between a wedding and a birthday party in a foreign country where you don't speak the language.

Gwenn had put a lot of time and attention into planning my niece's celebration and the weekend of events surrounding it, and I was excited. I was excited for my first trip since moving north—excited to be enveloped by the moist, warm Florida air that smells of hibiscus and hot mulch, greeting you as you step out of any sliding glass door that serves as a gateway from climate control to the natural world. I was excited to sit around a dining table with three generations of family I love and partake in raucous conversation that feels like verbal jigsaw puzzles, each of us so comfortable with the others that we find space to interject and finish one another's stories while laughing.

The winter had been tough in the snowy woods. I would later be teased for calling my house—seventy-five miles outside the city—"upstate," but to me, it was a completely different world. Food wasn't delivered, I couldn't walk to get a cup of coffee, and going to the supermarket was a three-hour round-trip outing. Technically upstate or not, there were so many storms my first winter in the country, and the more the plows scraped the road to move the dense, white carpet aside, the higher the mounds grew around us. Sam and I would step out into the dry, frigid, silent air at night to walk our boxer. With snow piles disguised as mountains looming above my five-foot-three frame and his six-foot-one head, it felt like walking in a white tunnel. All the change, plus being separated from my friends and family, was a challenge I carried in my bones. I didn't realize how encumbered I was until I got some space, perspective, and warm weather.

Sam and I had gotten to Florida before my dad and were in the hotel lobby when he, my stepmother Camilla, and my little sister Lia arrived. A panic-induced adrenaline coursed through my veins when I saw my dad, and it was immediately apparent that something was wrong. I noticed his clenched jaw and wide, unblinking eyes as he transitioned into a conversation, orchestrated with angry pointing and waving hand gestures that I couldn't hear from across the bustling hotel lobby. There was something in his expression—something different that I couldn't place—that told me this wasn't the man I remembered.

I approached him with a smile and hugged him, but he remained stiff and only offered a "hi." I tried to engage in some pleasantries about his trip and the details for the weekend, but I was cut short by his stare, which felt more as if it were peering through me at the framed photograph of palm trees on the wall behind where I stood than directed at me. He yelled at me about making sure I kept his first ex-wife and a cousin on Gwenn's maternal side of the family away from him for reasons he did not share. His frustration was directed at me even more when I tried to find out what had happened, as if asking for some context signified that I was minimizing how he was feeling. He bent down his six-foot-tall head to meet my gaze and commanded, "Just keep them away from me," in a deep, loud voice through unparted teeth before excusing himself to go to the hotel room where he was staying alone, apart from Camilla and Lia.

I looked to Camilla in his wake and met her eyes briefly before she shook her head in disgust, took Lia by the hand, and walked toward the elevators. I felt small, as if I had absorbed all of the tension emanating from my dad and Camilla and was slowly imploding from it. Logically, I knew I was not part of the problem and had done nothing wrong, but it was difficult not to internalize all of that confusing stress, take some ownership of it, and feel bad.

It's something I still struggle to stop myself from doing—assuming that no matter what is wrong, I am the cause of the problem. At that moment, I became a child again, blaming myself for my parents' fighting. Fortunately, options are the privilege of adulthood, so Sam and I decided to go get burritos instead of remaining in the middle of a conflict that was not ours.

Family gatherings often have an element of stress, particularly when there are strained relationships and ex-spouses involved, but my dad's demeanor in the lobby was beyond odd. He was enraged. I had seen him at uncomfortable family functions. I sat next to him at Gwenn's engagement party when he, in his sports coat with a tennis T-shirt beneath, drank too many sea breezes, danced like a scarecrow recently removed from its field post, and told everyone, on repeat how much he loved his daughters. He never wanted to be near his first ex-wife, Gwenn's mom, whom he had divorced about thirty-five years before the bat mitzvah, but he was typically diplomatic about it—or at least withheld his discomfort for the sake of others. Something had caused him to lose his diplomacy. Gone was his ability to pinball his way around people or conversations he wished to avoid, and in its place was an angry drill sergeant trying to yell the fear out of a newly admitted class of basic trainees.

My dad came from a long line of grudge holders, so his irritation with those he felt had wronged him was not a surprise. He often spoke privately of his distaste for certain family members, laying out his grievances in painstaking detail. What was surprising was his inability to temper his feelings for the sake of my niece or for Gwenn, who was trying to keep the peace and throw her daughter a nice party. He wouldn't pretend to be cordial. It was as if he had taken some drug that very specifically disinhibited the part of his brain that contained his frustrations, and they were all popping out like one of those practical joke cans full of fake coiled snakes. Thirty-five years' worth of unresolved issues spewed out onto the marble floor of a fancy reception hall.

When he wasn't actively fussing about someone, he was distracted—absent. I have one photo of my dad from that weekend: we were sitting at a large round table at the reception, and he was seated next to Camilla. Both wore their glasses, brims low on their noses, peering at their respective phones in their laps—like strangers on a subway. It embodied who they were that weekend: two people in separate worlds, uncomfortable and distant for different reasons.

My dad's behavior aside, I was happy—happy to be included in what felt like an otherwise functional family experience. When I went with Gwenn and my nieces to get our hair done for the party, I was glad to be with the girls. I was especially glad when my dad wanted to spend that time shopping with Sam. Perhaps the two would bond. They were both quiet, thoughtful men, so I couldn't imagine what they would talk about—probably sports.

While I was being tended to, they shopped for shorts and books. By the time my dad and Sam arrived back at the hotel, I was relaxed, with impeccably blown-out long blonde hair and nails manicured in lavender to match my niece's party color scheme. I was ready for a night of celebration.

"So, how was your day with my dad?" I asked with an exaggerated smile, chin perched atop my overlapped hands. My internal turmoil quickly returned. With a stoic look on his face, Sam said, "Something is wrong with your father." I was no longer a butterfly floating whimsically through the air, but one trapped on the ground beneath a child's cup.

He couldn't articulate his experience beyond the feeling that something was off. He appeared upset by what he had witnessed with my dad over the course of several hours of shopping. Sam was far from an alarmist, so for him to say anything at all meant it must have been obvious—and intrusive. I strove in vain to piece together what had occurred and why Sam was unwilling or unable to say more.

The rest of the weekend was externally uneventful. My dad acted more like himself than he had when he arrived in the hotel lobby, but something was clearly wrong. He typically thrived in the presence of his children and grandchildren—and the family we had pieced together for ourselves—but he spent the remainder of his unstructured time on the trip in his hotel room or alone.

When we were together, he was like a helium balloon one week after its intended use—still floating, but with less velocity and less air. He didn't initiate many conversations and responded with a muted nod or smile when engaged. It was as if expelling all his rage at the beginning of the weekend had left him depleted, just waiting for a chance to take a nap.

He wasn't angry at me, so I assumed he was just working through his own stuff. My own childhood had conditioned me to expect parents to do things separately, so I didn't recognize an issue when I spent time with Camilla and Lia at the pool while my dad remained elsewhere, in some unknown.

****

I try to recall details of the years when my dad was sick and come up with very little. My memory is fuzzy. The days, weeks, and months swirl around in a cyclone of distress and meld into one. The logical part of my brain was overtaken by the emotional part; the large academic library I envision in my head was vandalized—

the shelves overturned, books strewn across the ground, pages torn out.

In the weeks that followed the Florida trip, I kept talking to my dad, and he kept assuring me he was okay—politely at first, and then with increasing anger. I tried to make my check-ins sound casual. I didn't want to raise red flags—or rather, I didn't want to draw his attention to the red flags that were already there. "Good, everything is good," he'd respond when I asked about his day or his weekend. But when I asked how he was feeling, he would snap back, "I said I'm fine. Stop asking me that."

I couldn't pinpoint why the question bothered him. Did he genuinely believe he was fine, or was he deflecting? I snuck in calls to Camilla when he wasn't around. We had to be discreet—he would have been infuriated to learn we were talking about him, unconvinced by his fragile reassurances that he was actually okay. We knew he was not okay, and that it was high time we went over his head to figure out what was really going on.

She affirmed that his memory wasn't improving and that things were not status quo. She was concerned that the list of stored words on his phone continued to grow. She told me he had started spacing out when people talked to him, and that it was irritating—he never seemed to pay attention and always appeared distracted. She assumed it was something within his control, and she was justifiably frustrated.

By Father's Day, he seemed even further from the man I had previously known. There was less strength in his voice than just a couple of weeks earlier, and I noticed the moments when his mind drifted elsewhere. We had lunch and then walked around a few street fairs in the city. He bought us plastic cups of cut-up watermelon outside of Lincoln Center, as aspiring musicians played piano in the background. I tried to be agreeable and ate it—even though I don't like watermelon—just so I wouldn't upset him.

It was surprisingly hot for June, and I attributed his lethargy to the heat discharging from the buildings and the wool carpet of people spread beneath them. I remember the heat because I had gotten a nearly full-sleeve arm tattoo a month earlier and felt the need to wear a cardigan to shield my father from it. He had expressed a strong dislike of my tattoos, which, until that point, were in spots easily concealed from a father.

I loved my dad very much, and though that love didn't stop me from doing things he didn't like, it did motivate me to shield him from some of my decisions. So I walked around in the shadeless Manhattan sun in a sweater to protect my dad from me, waiting for him to say he'd had enough and wanted to go home. I should have known then that something was wrong. Not only did my dad not question my out-of-season wardrobe choice, but he also wore a long-sleeved shirt—with nothing to hide beneath it except some apparent malfunction in his internal thermometer.

THREE

Blurred views from the bottom of a pool

Oddly, my phone didn't ring much over the next couple of weeks. When my dad and I did speak, it was brief. He probably mentioned his memory being okay and referenced the little things that irritated him throughout the day. He was abrupt—not particularly interested in what either of us had to say.

I spoke to Camilla to fill in the gaps between what my father shared with me and what was actually happening. She said she had made him a doctor's appointment for mid-July, that whatever was going on was definitely not related to his cholesterol medication, and that she was worried.

Our conversations became more frequent. She and I didn't have a bad relationship, but we hadn't started out particularly close. My dad, in an attempt to recreate the family he lost, or maybe the one he never had, tried to push me and Camilla together faster than I was willing to go, and I resisted, maintaining a distance that felt safe at the time. One that gave me a small sense of control. When we were together, we chatted, laughed, and hugged, but there was only black matter between those in-person encounters. I was informed about her and Lia through my dad, who also relayed to her whatever details about me he deemed relevant. From a utilitarian standpoint, there hadn't been a need for more familiarity—until my father got sick.

As time went on, we began to connect the missing pieces for one another. There were discrepancies between what my dad revealed to each of us—and certainly between what he told me and what she experienced living with him during this cruel confusing time.

After nine months of derailing memory, erratic behavior, and internalized anxiety, my phone rang. The call came on a weeknight evening at the beginning of July. It was Sam's first day back at work in a year, and he was on a 3–11 shift, making it the first night I had to myself since we moved upstate.

My plan was to eat takeout, hang with my boxer, watch some television, go to bed early, and live a life reminiscent of my time in Queens. Back then, Sam and I worked opposite shifts, and I spent many evenings in contented solitude. I was excited to have a moment to catch my breath. I hadn't realized how much I valued time alone until it was taken away from me, and I was eager to return to being an independent person—someone who didn't have to consider what another human wanted to eat for dinner or watch on television. The universe had something else in mind. Fucking universe.

With a voice that barely hid her distress, Camilla explained that she had taken my dad to the doctor early; he was starting to zone out more often and for longer periods. She knew she couldn't wait. He had some tests, and imaging revealed a mass between the left temporal and occipital lobes of his brain. Doctors diagnosed him with glioblastoma multiforme (GBM) and scheduled him for brain surgery a couple of days later. GBM is a fast-growing and incurable form of brain cancer. What we thought was just him spacing out was actually a type of seizure called an absence seizure—aptly named for its characteristic lack of movement.

He was having seizures because the lump of cancer cells in his brain was growing and putting pressure on the limited real estate inside his skull. He wasn't distracted or having trouble focusing— his brain was short-circuiting as it fought against a foreign intruder. The temporal lobe, which sits below the frontal and parietal lobes, contains several sections responsible for speech, memory, and the connections between them. It made sense that the tumor, assaulting the essence of who my father was, did so by disrupting his ability to retrieve things—like the names of common words— from his long-term memory and produce them in speech.

My dad needed to undergo brain surgery to remove his tumor and slow the progression of his cancer. *Slow,*not stop. The doctors described the tumor as a tree with a tangle of roots. The tree could be cut down; however, the roots would remain, embedded in his brain, potentially lying dormant for some time before ultimately reanimating and continuing to grow. Life expectancy was not long, and the typical trajectory was a period of stability followed by gradual deterioration and, eventually, death. The doctors expressed optimism: there were clinical trials underway aimed at thwarting the tumor's return, and they explained that participating in a trial—combined with medication, chemotherapy, and radiation— would give my dad the best quality of life for the longest time. The doctors used words like "quality of life" and "comfortable" a lot to mask the underlying message—he was never getting better. There was no reset button. I don't blame them. I can't imagine how demoralizing it must be to spend your days delivering crushingly awful news and then watching families slowly incinerate in stress and grief for months or years until the embers stop glowing. I couldn't do it—definitely not with a straight face plastered with a smile.

Camilla and I discussed the logistics of what came next—partially because they needed to be discussed, and partially because it was easier than thinking about anything else. The conversation felt like a slow-motion video of a cannonball being launched into my stomach at close range. I had to keep it together on the phone. This tragedy was not more about me than Camilla, and I wasn't looking for her consolation in that moment. So we talked about facts. Next steps. Nuts and bolts. I would call Gwenn in Florida and let her know what was happening, and she would inform our other relatives. I would come down to the city the next day to see my dad and spend time with him before surgery. Then I'd go home, prepare for his post-surgery needs, and make hard phone calls to some of his friends. I'd figure out how to tell my friends and my supervisors at work. When it was all done, I would return to the city and accompany my dad home from the hospital.

It took me a minute to remember why Camilla wouldn't be around to take my dad home. Why would she be gone for something so important and scary? The answer was Lia.

Lia had turned ten while we were all in Florida. She was a lanky, curly-haired girl who often bounced around in leggings and a plain T-shirt. She loved the Jonas Brothers and Justin Bieber. Real kid stuff. She left for sleepaway camp not long before my dad's first doctor's appointment. It was a camp—like most were back then—where there was minimal contact with the outside world. Cell phones and social media weren't a thing. She had no idea what was happening at home. She had a chance—what would be her last chance—to be a little kid unencumbered by adult tragedy, and Camilla wanted to give her as much of that as possible.

She chose to let Lia stay at camp with her friends to accumulate her last uncomplicated childhood memories. The day my father was scheduled to come home from surgery fell in the middle of her family visiting weekend. Camilla planned to take one of her friends for the visit and to explain to Lia that Dad was sick but getting better, and that he would be home before she got there. She wanted to assure her that everything would be fine so Lia could enjoy the rest of her summer.

Here's one of those out-of-body moments. At the time, I didn't think much about the situation with Lia. I was preoccupied with my father, with family stuff, and with my own emotions. I didn't appreciate that Camilla was being pulled in multiple, conflicting directions—trying to do what was best for her daughter and for her husband. The exhaustion of it all is unimaginable. How hard that long drive to camp must have been, and how painful it must have been to leave her there. How did she find the strength to smile and try to convince a playful little girl that everything was going to be okay while knowing the opposite was true? I didn't think about what it was like to be a ten-year-old and watch your already-advanced-in-age father get very sick in front of you and completely change who he was. I didn't think of it much then, and I am eternally sorry for that—my continued repentance manifesting in the caretaking, love, and empathy I have for Lia, which will persist long after these words are read.

The evening I learned what was happening to my father was the first of many long nights to come. I stopped sleeping through the night without Benadryl. I'd often wake up at 2 a.m. and struggle to drift back off. I'd spend a couple of hours reading and then briefly return to bed before having to get up for work. It went on for months and was a new experience for me. My typical stress response was to turn inward and get tired, but my brain knew it couldn't outsleep what was coming and revolted with insomnia in the absence of other options—as if to convince me that I could figure out some perfect solution if I stayed awake long enough.

I didn't appreciate being involuntarily pulled from slumber, but I found peace in the darkness. I fantasized about being the last person on earth as I peered out my living room window into what looked like a black hole, as if doing so would shield me from hurt.

After making all the calls and finalizing the plans, I sat on the hardwood floor next to the full-wall limestone fireplace in my living room and cried. I was relieved to be alone. I had grown accustomed to keeping my emotions to myself, as I was convinced they were burdensome to others. Some of that restraint was self-imposed, and some of it was conveyed to me through the people I chose to be around—and was obligated to be around.

My life was largely filled with under-emoters and over-emoters. The over-emoters often overwhelmed me. They tended to express their genuine feelings in a way that felt melodramatic and disingenuous. Their needs created a vacuum that sucked everything out of the air, suffocating you with their severity. Everything was a big deal. Everything was felt with a full-body intensity, flung outward indiscriminately, without any awareness of whether others wanted—or were able—to receive it. There was no reading the room. They simply filled it.

I knew I never wanted to be perceived as a messy tornado of emotions tearing through someone else's day. This worked out well for the under-emoters, who viewed any display of feeling as unreasonable or unnecessary.

The under-emoters were uncomfortable with their own emotions, and other people's feelings were offensive to them. They told me I was too sensitive when I cried, that I was giving them a hard time when I was upset, that I was making too big a deal out of something, or that I was wrong for having my own idea of what my internal experience should be in a given situation. I didn't have to worry about any of the emotional derelicts that night—my brindle boxer, full of energy and acceptance, used her cool, damp black nose to sniff my tears and nudge my face without judgement.

I took the train into Grand Central Station to see my dad the next day; this would become my ritual over the course of his remaining years. It was my way to spend time with him and accompany him to doctor's appointments. I remember getting on the train that first morning, in the hours preceding rush hour, and being crammed next to a loud man in an ill-fitting suit. He was wearing too much cologne and gulping down an energy drink at a time of day that suggested he was probably a douchebag. Despite the small space, he pulled out his laptop and phone and began loudly conducting business that was both physically and mentally intrusive. I was angry. I thought, *"This asshole gets to live, and my dad is sick?"*

I knew it was a crappy way to think, and honestly, out of character for me, but this was a new situation—one I didn't know how to handle. I was generally capable of solving my own problems. The universe had taught me that if I worked hard and persevered, challenges were manageable and could be overcome. Then, it decided I needed to learn something else: inexplicably bad things happen, and those need to be navigated too.

After the first angry train ride, I sought comfort in public transportation to Manhattan and Grand Central Station. There was a methodical cadence to the trips that gave me a sense of security—a false sense of control. On the train, I would stare out the window, listen to music, and mentally prepare myself for the hours ahead. When I arrived at Grand Central, I would buy an overpriced but delicious coffee and a decadent pastry to enjoy on the rest of the journey to see my dad.

Grand Central itself was paradoxically soothing. The massive train station is chaotic, filled with people rushing in no predictable pattern. It was like trying to cross the street in Rome. Hidden in the disorder, though, was peace for me. The building is so vast that individual sounds disappear. There's a general muffled hum that comes with movement, but it was quiet in the same way that holding your breath and sinking to the bottom of a pool is quiet. I feel my blood pressure lowering just thinking about it—which is helpful, since thinking about and writing all the other parts of this story do the opposite.

Once off the train and out in the city air, I'd press play on my music and weave through the nameless bodies on the sidewalk, living their distinct lives as I walked to NYU. Most people looked like they were going to work or school. Very few appeared to be headed to sit in a hospital room with their Greek tragedy lives. Very few seemed to be repeating *"I'm okay, I'm okay, I'm okay"* over and over again in their heads, in cadence with their steps, as I was, walking the twenty blocks downtown.

****

I saw my dad on one of those white hospital blankets knitted from some kind of stain-repellent cotton string before his surgery, and we didn't discuss anything serious. We made small talk in a hospital bed, hours before he was to have his skull cut open and a section of his brain removed. He did not look like a patient as he sat up with the aid of his adjustable mattress, a white pillow halo circling his face. We chatted as if I were visiting him at his office or as if we were sitting on his living room couch. We talked about the July weather outside his sealed hospital window. He told me he felt good, offering a smile he hoped would convince me.

During my visit, he took a phone call to give one of his former students a job recommendation, never mentioning that he was in a hospital on the brink of major surgery. That's who my dad was—cool, composed, and always focused on what needed to be done. He wasn't sure what shape he'd be in post-surgery, but he wanted to make sure he expressed what a good person his student was and what a valuable employee he would be. I can see him lying in that bed in that white room, his pale hospital gown dotted with small blue geometric shapes, smiling as he spoke to me about being a job reference. He was happy to be doing something for someone else. Happy to have a distraction from his impending situation that reminded him he was still good. Still useful.

My memory of the pre-surgery time in the hospital with my dad is spotty, in the typical way that time tends to wear things down. I see what happened over the next few years as discrete moments, like light through a pinhole camera. I didn't stay in the city for my dad's surgery. I went home. I spent the day getting the oil changed in my car, because that was very important, and cooking food to bring to him when he got out of the hospital.

As I write this, I ask myself, why didn't you stay? Why was going home so necessary? I probably needed to be at my house for my dog, but I also probably didn't yet understand what was happening. I was still under the false belief that things happen, then we reset, and then things go back to the way they were. I was unable to project outward to an experience I had not encountered before. Not yet able to understand that my big picture was not going to recalibrate and that my priorities would inadvertently shift. I don't fault myself for it. None of us can predict how the hurdles we encounter will change us with much accuracy.

So, I stood in a patch of grass outside my car dealer, talking to Camilla about my dad's brain surgery as I waited for my regular car maintenance to be done. That night, I focused on cooking for my dad and Camilla. I felt helpless and needed to do something to feel in control, and food is my typical go-to. Food, and conversations about food, had tethered my dad and me to one another so often over the years, and on the eve of his surgery, I searched for old habits to maintain the connection—to feel close to him in familiar ways.

I didn't know what to expect when I returned to the hospital. Brain surgery—the most serious-sounding of surgeries, second only to heart surgery. My dad was lucid when I got there. He seemed good. Surprisingly good. He recognized me, knew where he was, and spoke to me in full sentences about his doctors and the nurses. He mentioned how everyone was struck by how youthful he looked for his age, and how impressed they were by his physical condition. He often boasted about the positive feedback he received from others about his appearance, and while it was on a short list of qualities I found irritating, I smiled, comforted to see that some part of his essence remained post-surgery.

A gauze bandage was wrapped around his head, the kind you'd see in movies when someone sustains a minor head injury. Gauze. It minimized the significance of what had happened and lulled me into falsely believing that things were fine. Serious conditions require contraptions and braces, not gauze. How could someone have brain surgery and be okay enough to leave the hospital four days later with nothing but gauze around their head? Sam and I waited for my dad to be cleared to leave, and it felt like forever. I was anxious to get through the part of the day where I had to navigate my dad back to his apartment. It was one of the first tasks I had been given where there were massive consequences if I messed it up, and I lacked the confidence to assure myself that I wouldn't.

His discharge paperwork came with a long list of medications and extremely detailed instructions—specific times, exact dosages, and precise conditions for when they were to be taken. There were endless warnings about falling, moving his head too quickly, and the dangers of even a minor head injury. I wished he had a helmet instead of gauze. There were large plastic jugs he needed to pee in, and in a very specific way, as part of his clinical trial.

Knowing and conveying important information to my dad about his aftercare was the most adult responsibility I had been tasked with, and I felt unprepared, like I had skipped the class that taught you how to successfully navigate someone home from the hospital but showed up for the final exam without my number two pencil. Sam and I stood in the hospital pharmacy so long that my knees started to throb. I shifted my weight between my feet, eyes locked on the bench in the lobby where my dad sat and waited for us. We eventually left with bags of pill bottles and large urine containers that made us appear as if we had gone on the world's greatest shopping spree in a medical supply store. My heart beat quicker as I thought about what was waiting for us on the other side of the hospital's large glass doors.

We had to take a cab to my dad's apartment across town. I was anxious, not just about getting him home, but about bringing him into the world again—and protecting him. He was vulnerable. He depended on me now, the way I had once depended on him as a child, but the stakes felt so much higher. I didn't have a gaping head wound as a child, and there was a strong probability that I wouldn't fall, have a seizure, or die if I did something as simple as tripping. I also fully understood that my parents were in charge and that I had to listen to them. Those were the rules. The same rules did not apply to a grown man being tended to by his not-so-grown-up daughter. I could not simply tell my dad what to do; he needed to agree.

I thought about the long and boring leadership trainings I'd sat through at work, where I was taught that sometimes the best idea was the one that got the most buy-in from your team, even if it wasn't the objectively best one. I needed my dad's buy-in, but the margin for error in a less-than-ideal plan had to be small; the consequences of a misstep were massive. I was a tightrope walker on a greased line, trying to make my way over a pool full of broken glass, and my dad, brain damage or not, was stubborn and an independent thinker—a difficult employee to manage, indeed.

We made it into a cab, and I winced at every bump and sharp turn. I hadn't realized how much road repair was needed in the city until I had to ride in a car with a man whose head seemed as delicate as a Fabergé egg. My dad didn't object as I guided him into the elevator and down the hall to his apartment door. He insisted on using the key himself to open the door and escorted himself to his unspoken spot on the couch.

He wanted to nap when we got home and relented when I insisted he keep the door to his room open. In the living room, I tried to decode his medication list and realized he needed an over-the-counter stool softener in addition to everything else that had to get filtered through his body. Sam and I walked five blocks to the drugstore, where I found what he needed and also picked up some of his favorite treats from my childhood—probably more for my comfort than his.

Entenmann's Rich Frosted Donuts and plain Lay's potato chips were my dad's only indulgences when I was growing up, and it felt important to have them, as if they were part of some voodoo doctor's concoction to make my dad well again. To tether him to the man he used to be. The cancer-free man who would lie in bed, his long, slender legs crossed at the ankle, watching television, eating a donut or a portion of potato chips displayed on a white paper towel laid out on the sheet beside him like a small one-man picnic.

I carried the plastic bag of donuts, potato chips, and stool softener back to his apartment. I felt like I was fully submerged underwater, looking out at a blurry world I no longer recognized.

My default in stressful situations, besides getting tired, is having a stomachache and becoming as task-oriented as possible. I revert to my childhood self—focusing on homework, on the steps needed to reach some predictable and logical conclusion. When Sam and I got back to my dad's apartment with all the snacks and medications, I suggested that I stay over to help him manage everything and keep him company. He politely declined at first, then with a "NO" that was of an intensity I rarely saw in him since I entered adulthood. He insisted he didn't need a babysitter—even if he actually did. I let go with the hesitance of a parent releasing a toddler on the verge of his first steps. I made lists of all his medications and the times they needed to be taken, and Sam programmed alarms into his phone for each of them. I left hoping

I had not made a mistake, but realizing I did not have much of a choice.

I had long ago adopted a *"what is my goal here?"* perspective with my father. My goal then, as it often was with him, was to do what I needed to do to maintain our relationship. When I was twenty-two, my dad called me and told me that Camilla, whom he had previously insisted did not want children, was pregnant. The world slowed down after I got the news. My dad paused in seeming anticipation of an upset rant that ultimately did not come. I had a lot of mixed feelings about the prospect of a half-sibling who would be twenty-three years my junior, but in that moment, I realized it would not serve me to be angry about it or to force my complicated feelings on anyone else.

My dad and his wife's decision was not about me, and I could choose to adapt to it or not. I did not want to lose my father, and I did not want to feel angry. A tiny, faultless baby deserved to enter a family that loved and cared for her, no matter the circumstances. So, I asked questions and expressed support. He was relieved that I did not laugh at him and hang up, as Gwenn reportedly did in response to the news, according to him. We moved on in our ever-changing dynamic, and while there were certainly tenuous moments in the months to follow, none of them were because I was angry about something I could not control and had no right trying to.

I left the city believing that the toll staying with him would take on our relationship was not worth the cost of doing so. I called him every couple of hours through the evening and the next morning until Camilla joined him at home. It was the first of many hard choices I encountered over the next three years.

While my dad seemed generally okay immediately after surgery, he did not return to his previous baseline. The dad I knew never came back. The version of my dad that replaced the father I had known for thirty-three years was slower, quieter. He initially thought he could still work and would ultimately begin driving again—both of which turned out to be untrue.

The pre- and post-cancer changes in my dad felt so extreme because he was an athlete. Professional duties aside, he spent much of his free time in an active state. His favorite sustained activity was rollerblading by the beach. Even after moving to Manhattan, he'd drive to Long Island and "blade," as he embarrassingly called it, for twenty miles at a time. There were days when he would drive us both to the beach, and we would start out together—him on his blades, and me running. He'd go forever and be calmly waiting for me at the car as I wrapped up my three-mile run, huffing and red-faced. When he couldn't zip around on eight wheels, he was in the gym or on the elliptical machine in his house.

In the city, he purchased an adult-sized scooter and would weave through half of Manhattan to make sure he got his exercise in, no matter how much Lia and I teased him about the optics. He believed he could outmaneuver the aging process, and it seemed to be working. He didn't drink, nor did he eat red meat, and he rarely ate cheese. He was healthy and energetic. At sixty-five, he retired from coaching and decided he wanted to travel. He went to London and Paris by himself for their Tennis Open events. He was planning on Australia next.

The healthy version of my father cared about his appearance—about looking cool. My boyfriend after college used to call my dad "The Fonz" because of all the leather jackets and jeans. My dad took a lot of pride in his hair, which was a black dandelion puff on his head in his youth and evolved into a neatly shaped coiffe of salt-and-pepper waves as he got older. He started getting lowlights after he met Camilla to look younger and help close the near fifteen-year age gap between them. Once, I accompanied him to his hair appointment, and I can still see him sitting in a Long Island basement hair salon, in the home of a friend of his, with one of those shower caps with holes in it on his head, as tufts of hair were pulled through with a crochet hook to be darkened. He insisted the very silly process was worth the results and was not ashamed of the steps he took to maintain his good looks.

After brain surgery, all his concern about his physical appearance evaporated—not in that "I-have-gone-through-something-hard-and-no-longer-care-about-superficialities" way, but in a "I-no-longer-have-any-sort-of-awareness-of-my-physical-form-in-this-world" way. He purchased a straw cowboy hat patterned like a wicker chair to cover up his head wounds after surgery, and continued to wear the hat as his hair began falling out in clumps from chemotherapy.

The hat was objectively silly on my father as he ambled about the streets of Manhattan in track pants and a sweatshirt with his new, reanimated-corpse walking cadence. He was adamant about not wanting to wear anything different, even after the hat began to deteriorate and develop holes in the indentations cowboys use to take their hats on and off. He had been a baseball hat guy before surgery, and I longed for him to be one again, both for the aesthetics and the logistics. The cowboy hat was clunky, like a purse without a strap, and difficult to manage while sitting at a restaurant table. It also struggled with aerodynamics, which created functional hurdles. I remember chasing the tattered hat up West End Avenue after a gust of wind lifted it from his head, and the pleased look I received in exchange for rescuing it as he repositioned it atop his remaining hair.

He began wearing the same outfit every day. I think he had a few versions of it that he alternated between, but it was the same black, wide-bottomed athletic pants and the same blue long-sleeved shirt embroidered with the Queens College Men's Tennis logo—the same shirt he had on when he helped me move.

When he first married Camilla, he complained that the speed with which she did laundry screwed up his shirt rotation. He was flustered when he found himself wearing the same three shirts from the top of the pile, as he didn't have the opportunity to reach the shirts at the bottom—as if some unspoken rule prohibited him from pulling a shirt from the middle of the stack.

Not only did he no longer care about the redundancy of his outfits, but it became very important to him to wear the same thing—his sick-person uniform. He was probably trying to streamline the cognitive energy required by daily tasks while also dealing with the kind of apathy about physical appearance that only brain surgery can conjure, but I didn't have that insight at the time. In the moment, all I saw was how much my dad had metamorphosed, and all I felt was how much I did not like it.

My dad also deteriorated mentally. He used to be sarcastic and prided himself on a Jerry Seinfeld-esque wit that endlessly amused him. He'd get this open-mouthed smirk after saying something he thought was particularly funny, and would shrug his shoulders, raise his hands, and bob his head while repeating the one-liner if his audience did not pick up on the smile and give him some reaction.

He spoke slowly, quietly, and rarely joked following his surgery. As time passed, his motivation to do the things he previously enjoyed dissipated. Gone were the days when he longed to venture to the beach or travel to see Gwenn and his grandchildren in Florida. I offered to accompany him on trips to the Hamptons to visit a close friend, or to fly with him for family visits, and he always declined, assuring me that he would see the people he wanted to see and do the things he wanted to do when he felt better. I didn't dare to question what would happen if he did not feel better. This might be as good as it got. I didn't want to be negative, though I suspected I was just being realistic. I kept my thoughts to myself and nodded in agreement that the plans could wait.

I began spending more time with him, coming down to the city more frequently for reasons other than attending appointments. I seemed to have a calming effect on him, and it felt good to have an assumed purpose. He started getting annoyed with other people in his life arbitrarily. He lost patience, was sensitive to noise, and could not contain his frustration. He demanded silence in the house and chastised visitors when he believed a voice was too loud or too high-pitched, turning his head to the side and closing his eyes to block out rational points—that while people could speak more softly, it was asking a lot for someone to alter their timbre.

He never really got upset with me. I was quiet, our interactions were time-limited, and I did not challenge him on anything. We bonded over sitting silently and saying nothing at all. Infusion appointments would last for hours. Sometimes we would chat; other times, we sat without speaking as he faded in and out of sleep, perking up to ask me what music I was listening to when he saw I had put my headphones on. I had no expectations of him and no ulterior motives other than just being with him as much as I could for as long as I could.

Food remained our nonverbal communication, the quiet connection that kept us tethered to one another no matter how sick he got. Even as his body failed him, our routine around meals felt like the only time when he was still the father I had once known. He would be nauseous from all the chemo, radiation, and other drugs pumping through him, but still wanted to figure out lunch. He cared if I was eating and what he was eating. We would discuss menus and options, decide what time the food should be ordered, and when I should go pick it up. Me finishing a meal was validating for him and seemed to make him proud that he had chosen a good restaurant. He was eating much less and spun his limited intake into a positive, saying he was glad he could get a second meal out of whatever he ordered—having it for dinner that night or lunch the next day. I would usually pick up banana pudding from Magnolia Bakery for him at Grand Central Station, and he would have some for dessert even on the queasiest of days. We settled into a mostly predictable rythm—a timeline where the tick marks were MRIs, deli trips, and banana pudding.

Sometimes after appointments, he wanted to go to Fairway, a supermarket on the East Side of Manhattan that he believed had an excellent selection of cut-up fruit and small containers of potato salad. While I loved a good solo trip to Fairway—for non-produce and prepared food reasons—I hated going there with my dad.

Over the years, I have felt guilt at various times about a number of things that transpired during my dad's sickness, but Fairway was not one of them. I obliged in taking him there because it was important to him, but it meant walking several city blocks with him, watching him maneuver down a steep escalator, and standing by supportively as he floated through supermarket aisles, generally unaware of the people around him or the natural patterns of foot traffic. The trips took forever, despite him ultimately getting the same small collection of items. His vision had worsened from the surgery and treatments, and he needed me to read him labels and ingredients. If I wandered too far from him within the aisle, distracted by some item that caught my interest, he'd yell to me, "Amanda, come here. Tell me what's in this," and I would scurry to him, cheeks glowing with my childhood embarrassment.

I'm not complaining about having to help my brain-damaged father in a supermarket. I would have helped him do anything. The hypervigilance and anxiety I experienced during those trips were intolerable. I worried about everything: him falling, him getting injured, someone saying something to him—for being slow or standing aimlessly somewhere. Thinking about it makes my stomach hurt. There was so much vulnerability to protect him from—without overstepping and adding myself to the list of people who annoyed him.

The supermarket trips felt unbearable and unnecessary— like electing to skip through a room of open bear traps with the lights off. Groceries could be delivered. Other people could bring him things. I didn't realize that, for my dad, the trips were his autonomy. How it must have felt almost normal to go to a store and make choices about the foods he wanted to purchase and eat. He insisted on going to the store because it was a snapshot in time that reminded him what it was like to be well—and he was not yet ready to surrender to the opposite. I get it now, even if I didn't then.

FOUR

Tiny huge moments

We learned our new roles and played them well once the initial shock of my dad's illness subsided. For a brief period—one that feels like a soapy-eyed blink and was actually about five or six months long—life seemed okay. Though his baseline had dropped to unrecognizable levels, my dad's health stabilized. The surgery and treatments had slowed the progression of his cancer, and his MRI appointments moved to every three months. During the first year of his illness, I had been afraid to travel too far from New York out of fear that something might happen to him. With some space to breathe, Sam and I decided to spend a long Halloween weekend in Florida with Gwenn, my brother-in-law, and my nieces. I ached for time with my relatives that centered around costumes and plastic skeletons rather than the actual things that scared me in the middle of the night.

I visited my long-distance family every couple of months during my unencumbered late teens and twenties, so the year and a half I spent away felt very long. The trip was important. We needed to nurture our relationship amidst all the stress and adversity of my dad's illness, with the subtext being that I wanted to make sure we didn't all fall apart once my dad was gone. I loved my family and didn't want to lose anyone else. During the weekend, serious conversations were replaced with trick-or-treating and spooky-themed dinners. My niece painted my and Sam's faces. We all laughed together, and I began to feel confident that we would be okay—no matter what was waiting to meet us at the end of my dad's road.

In the distance that grew between the doctors' visits and the melancholy trips, I started thinking about having children. Long train rides left a lot of space for introspection, and I found my mind drifting to my relatives. The connection between Gwenn and my nieces felt more important. They had become the family anchor—the sun the rest of my bloodline revolved around—and I wanted to be a bigger part of that. I thought about how nice it would feel to come home from a hard day and be met by an entourage of people who loved me and could dilute sadness just by being there. I wanted to create my own universe and have that universe interconnect with one I already valued. I imagined family vacations at large beach rental houses, full of chaotic laughter during the day and deep conversations about love and our lives at night.

In my early twenties, I was pretty sure I did not want kids. I was fairly grossed out by the thought of another person growing in my body, and that faded into worry about the rest of it—the responsibility of sustaining another human's life for a prolonged period in a way that did not cause damage. I was still in grad school, and it all seemed like too much. I wanted to be selfish, to spend time with friends and do whatever I wanted in the small bits of free time I scavenged from academic responsibilities. Sam and I were on the same ambivalent page, though he was sure that what he called my "crazy woman instinct" would kick in at some point and I'd change my tune. Once married, our conversations about never having children rolled into a hypothetical "if we have kids" and an eventual "when we have kids." But no plans were made, and that felt fine—until my dad got sick.

My dad's illness did not trigger some hormonal tidal wave that ignited an evolutionarily driven childbearing instinct. But it did make me reconsider what it meant to be part of a family—and the benefits of healthy human connection that were biologically bound. I increasingly appreciated the importance of having a support network that was going through the same thing I was, rather than just empathizing from a distance. I felt more connected to my dad, Camilla, and Lia, and I wanted that world to expand. I wanted to give the family something happy to focus on. I wanted my dad to have the chance to be a grandfather again.

I came home from one of my dad's city doctor visits and told Sam, "If we're going to have children, I'd like to do it sooner rather than later so my dad can be a grandfather."

"That's not a reason to have children," he responded—and the conversation was over. A door slammed in my face for an undetectable reason.

I knew how Jehovah's Witnesses must feel when traveling from home to home to peddle their religion. I felt myself retreating within. I felt small. I didn't think I was being unreasonable, and I was unsure why he was taking such a hard line—making a unilateral decision on something we had talked around for years. We didn't discuss it again, but I didn't stop thinking about it. I decided I wanted a baby. I was ready to invest my time and energy in something other than my marriage and to feel deeply connected to someone other than Sam, with whom I wasn't feeling very deeply connected. Life stressors can push people together or tear them apart, and we had been trending toward the latter. I didn't think a baby could bring us closer, but I do understand how easy it could be to develop that delusion—that two people are capable of pushing their individual needs and issues aside to join forces for something greater than themselves. I saw having a baby as an ally, something that would take the place of a disconnected marriage. Something that would always be there.

One day in early spring, I decided it was time. Sam was sitting on the couch in our den when I told him I was going to stop my birth control and that I thought we should start trying. He agreed— or didn't disagree—responding instead with a diverted-eye-contact silence that had come to feel familiar in our relationship. In prior instances, I would have been disappointed by the reaction and would have stayed stagnant until I got a definitive answer from him about what we should do. In prior instances, I would have interpreted the absence of a response as a "no" and gotten quiet and apathetic myself. The baby conversation felt different. For the first time, I took action without waiting for his overt approval. It was a pivotal moment in our relationship. We were going to have a baby because I said so.

I started thinking about how life was going to change. *"I bet I'll be one of those people who gets pregnant as soon as birth control stops,"* I thought. Why wouldn't I? I lived a healthy lifestyle, filled with exercise and free from the kinds of things that people can superficially associate with infertility: drugs, alcohol, smoking, health conditions. I had avoided them all and was confident that things would go right, and that baby-making would reaffirm my embedded notions about life: want something, work for it, get it.

Much to my surprise, I was not one of those people and was yet again confronted with a situation where my logic did not prevail.

I started to get worried after about six months of casual trying. Getting pregnant became an unsolvable puzzle. I asked the internet endless hypothetical questions about my body functions, food, and timing. I figured there was some key piece of information I was missing. The more I learned, the longer my list of over-the-counter supplements became, and the more sweet potatoes I started eating.

A friend of mine who had struggled with fertility told me about ovulation strips, so I bought some from Amazon, along with tiny cups to pee in. She taught me her process of testing my urine every morning and night. I taped the used sticks to an index card and wrote the dates and times beneath them, watching the strips get darker each day until they signaled that I was ovulating.

My bathroom was full of cups, tape, test sticks, and index cards—it was my worst adult science fair project. It felt nice to have a tangible thing to focus on, even though that tangible thing was not working and was very unromantic. Sex became a stressful function of a larger goal rather than an intimate act between two people who cared for one another.

Afterward, I'd lie in bed alone with my legs above my head for up to twenty minutes—another suggestion from the endless internet remedies. There was minimal reciprocal communication in the house at that time. I was like a flagger directing obedient traffic. I never knew how Sam felt about the regimented sex, the struggles with pregnancy, about me, or about us. A couple more months went by, and it was decided that we should see a fertility doctor. We both assumed nothing was wrong and figured it would be nice to get some assurances.

A recurring theme in the next steps of my journey in and out of pregnancy was feeling completely unprepared, small, and out of control because of it. There were lengthy questionnaires to complete before the first appointment, and once there, the casual conversation I had anticipated quickly transformed into me, in a gown, on an observation table preparing for an intravaginal ultrasound.

In the months to come, intravaginal ultrasounds would become routine, but the first one was not. For those of you who have not had the experience, imagine a video-equipped ultrasound probe being inserted into your body by a stranger in a strange place while your partner and another unfamiliar nurse look on. It was intrusive and unexpected, and the casual conversation occurring around me while it was happening seemed surreal. I felt like a violated specimen, nothing more.

When it was done and I was dressed, Sam and I sat in a consultation room with the doctor while residual lubricant leaked out of my vagina, through my underpants and dress, and onto the chair I was seated in. The confidence I had acquired as an adult professional slipped from my body and onto that upholstered chair. I hated all of it. I felt inept, as though I was being excluded from the club of normal personhood on too many fronts—and I couldn't do anything about it. My dad was going to die, and I couldn't have a baby.

I smiled and nodded while the doctor talked about timelines, subsequent appointments, and bloodwork. I never realized that having a baby could be so complicated or require so much coordination. I was so unprepared, like a crumpled-up piece of paper someone realized they still needed and tried to flatten out. The experience—everything, from the doctor to the failed attempts—made me feel damaged in a way I hadn't encountered since I was a teenager.

In high school, I often felt insecure, sad that I wouldn't get chosen for one thing or another, but I worked through it by focusing on academics to ensure I did everything in my power to evade that feeling. I made myself valuable, and very often, I did get chosen. In infertility, I was that teenager again, waiting by my phone instead of going out with my friends, hoping for a callback that never came. I had done all the work but was still getting left behind.

Inexplicably, between my first messy appointment and the next, and without any additional unpleasant tests or procedures, I got pregnant. There was a faint line on a pregnancy test the day before Sam and I left to meet Gwenn and her family in Boston. I couldn't believe it. It seemed impossible that I had gotten pregnant doing the same things we had been doing, with no change other than a doctor's appointment that felt like date rape.

We didn't trust the line. We wondered if it was too early to tell and decided to say nothing, testing again when we got home. The trip was not the trip of two people thrilled about embarking on family life together. We were distant, barely talking. I retreated into myself further and began wondering what the future would be like and how I would protect a child from spaces full of jagged noiselessness. I tested again when we got home, and I was indeed pregnant.

I started feeling sick quickly, which everyone said was a good sign. I was mildly nauseous all the time, finding solace in saltines and ginger candies. We bought parenting books, and I began sending Sam emails about my fears and desires. I felt my perspective shifting rapidly. Behaviors and mannerisms that I had previously tolerated from my partner were starting to seem intolerable in the face of parenting. I worried he might not be able to change, or that we wouldn't adapt, and I would be left to figure it out on my own.

The microscopic being growing inside me became a magnifying glass on my marriage. His unresolved issues, our unresolved issues as a couple, and his general inability to communicate about any of it now seemed like a dark, spiked mountain looming over us—one I could not ignore. I felt a strong urge to shield my barely formed baby from generational trauma and was not convinced that Sam would be able to do it, even if he wanted to. My attempts to raise what felt like important issues were met with a deafening silence that pulsed through my body and resonated in my skull like the sound of my own heartbeat. I channeled my worries into early morning diatribe emails to Sam, which were read and often responded to with "I knows" and "I'm sorrys," but with no ideas about how to remedy what was wrong.

In lighter moments, we began talking about names, room colors, and all the hypotheticals that come with such a huge life change. We downloaded one of those apps that compares the baby's size to a food item each week and describes what's happening developmentally. We had our first ultrasound, and things started to feel real. We smiled as we looked at the first fuzzy black-and-white pictures of the tiny being we were creating, and a small crack of light shone on my parenting worries. Maybe it would all be okay. I was in awe of the speck of a thing in my body that would eventually become a human. I assumed the hard part must be over. I had gotten pregnant, and the only thing left to do was wait for the oven timer to go off while steering clear of cold cuts, runny eggs, and soft cheese.

We told people early—too early—with the nonchalance of people falsely confident that things would work out. I was excited to tell my dad. His life had become mundane and muted, and I wanted to give him something that would turn the volume back up. I wrote the announcement in his birthday card when we met him for dinner, surprising him with something else to celebrate in his apartment before we went out. He was ecstatic. He gave me a hug that emanated pride and relief—not the frail, wilted ones to which I had become accustomed. It was the hug of a man who, for a brief moment, forgot he was nauseous, constipated, and had brain cancer. It was the hug of a man full of life and optimism. We were all so excited to have something good. It was one of the last times I saw a genuine smile cross his face.

My dad reverted to whatever version of his dad role he could harness during my pregnancy. He started calling me more often and asking how I was feeling. I had broken through his self-focused misery, and he stepped back into life. One Friday evening, I drove into the city for dinner with him and Camilla. Lia was at a friend's party, and Sam was working, so it was just the three of us—something that hadn't happened since before Lia was born. For the first time in a long while, I felt like I had a starring role in a family unit, rather than my usual walk-on part. We shuffled to the restaurant with his arm on my shoulders.

At dinner, Camilla talked to me about being a mom and what she liked and didn't like about becoming a parent at the older end of the fertility pendulum. It was the kind of advice that leaves you feeling warm and cared for. My life felt like it was falling back into place. Maybe my dad's relentless positivity was working after all. Maybe things would be okay for a while. For two and a half months, they were. And then they weren't.

My dad had an MRI scheduled in September, and I did not attend the appointment due to worsening morning—nay, all-day—sickness and concerns about being in a hospital while pregnant. Camilla called me afterward and told me that, fourteen months later, the tree roots in my dad's brain had reanimated into cancer.

The doctors, waning in their optimism, proposed one final clinical trial. It wasn't a cure but a last hope to extend his time. He could live up to a year. The average was thirty weeks. He tried to stay positive. There was something good to focus on, and he wasn't feeling worse. We continued on.

Every October, there was a Sunday when the clinical staff at the forensic psychiatric hospital where I worked were required to come to work for a special event—Family Day. On Family Day, the supportive relatives of whichever patients still had living relatives—many of them had injured or murdered a relative—could visit the hospital for the afternoon, enjoy a boxed lunch and some entertainment, and meet with the patient's treatment team members. Most clinical staff hated Family Day, as it often coincided with the weekend in the fall when the best Hudson Valley activities were happening. There were festivals and craft fairs, all trying to capitalize on what could be the last warm hours of the outdoor event season before it was time to hunker down for winter. I was not yet a jaded state worker and did not mind Family Day. I had formed relationships with some of my patients and their families and looked forward to chatting in person.

Our hospital was an ominous compound composed of many old brick buildings connected by sidewalks bordered with tall fences topped with coils of razor wire that resembled very large and very dangerous stretched-out slinkies. I was walking down a short path between the building that housed the gym and the building that housed my office, on my way to forage for a snack, when I felt a sharp pain in my abdomen—one I can only imagine feels similar to being stabbed in the stomach. The pain was intense enough to stop me in my tracks and bend me over, resolving itself after a couple of seconds. Once mobile again, I took the elevator to my office instead of walking up the four flights of stairs, which was my norm, pregnant or not.

I wondered about that pain. Was it a typical part of pregnancy related to my organs shifting and my body stretching? Should I not have worn high heels to Family Day? I called the answering service for my OB-GYN, who asked me some questions but didn't provide satisfactory information. Was I bleeding? No. Was I still in pain? No. Then they pulled out the not-scientifically-validated pain scale—the picture you see in doctor's offices with a smiley face on one end and a frowny face on the other. They asked me how bad the pain was on a scale from one to ten, and I guessed a six while realizing that I had no idea how to conceptualize that pain in a single-digit number that made sense.

I have a high pain tolerance. When my sternum was fractured in high school after I was crushed between a metal barrier and several people at a Hole concert, I stayed at the concert. I went to school the next day. I went to work. The sharp pregnancy pain wasn't as bad as the concert injury pain, and it certainly didn't last as long. Prior to my Family Day experience, I hadn't thought much about the pain scale, and now I find it deeply troubling. I'd give it a nine out of ten on a scale of uselessness. The pain scale is relative. My six could be someone else's nine. I wonder how a medical professional makes decisions based on a subjective number that represents nothing more than a person's perception of an experience.

I've shared many rants about the pain scale over the years and continue to grumble about it every time I see that chart with the stupid faces separated by a random line hanging in a doctor's office. I still wonder what information the on-call nurse garnered from my pain scale answer. Probably nothing. What is the trigger to action—nine? Ten? I'd love to know so I can ensure I say the correct thing the next time I believe I'm in need of medical attention. I've been told that doctors and nurses might not take my experiences seriously because I often present as calm and unfazed regardless of what's happening to me. Do I need to scream more? Should I cry? If so, why is our medical care so reliant on irrelevant numbers and melodrama?

The on-call nurse I spoke to on Family Day told me I could go to the ER if I was worried, but that things were probably fine since the pain was gone, and that I should call back or head to the hospital if anything seemed worse. Things did not get worse. I went home, told Sam about the weird pain, and then forgot about it. I still felt nauseous and tired. Nothing seemed to have changed, and I went about my business munching on crackers.

A week later, Sam planned to go to our friend's birthday party on Long Island, and I was going to stay home. I didn't feel up to the drive—particularly since it would have meant being out late on a Sunday night—and was content to have an evening alone. I made myself a salad for dinner and was about to settle in for an early night on the couch when I noticed a couple of light pink blood spots in my underwear. I debated with myself about whether the spots were actually there, removing my underwear and bringing it close to my face for further inspection. I decided that the stain was not an unfortunate product of my anxious mind and battled myself further over what to do about it. I pulled towards denial, to wanting to eat my salad, watch tv, and forget what I saw, but the part of me that houses gut instincts would not let it go.

I called the doctor, and they again told me I should go to the ER if I was worried. I was learning what a mystery pregnancy was. The doctors and nurses seemed to have few answers that were more concrete than guesswork. I paused for a moment in that space between denial and action and decided I should go to the hospital to make sure everything was okay. I called Sam mid-drive, told him what was happening, and he turned around and met me at the ER.

I was surprised that he wanted to meet me, and he was surprised that I was surprised. I was used to him telling me I made too big a deal out of things, to him downplaying my perspective, telling me I was giving him a hard time when I raised a concern about him staying out too late or doing things that made me uncomfortable. His decision to come to the hospital signaled that something serious could indeed be happening. I couldn't ignore what he couldn't ignore.

The ER was eerily quiet for a rainy Sunday afternoon—nothing like what I had seen on TV or experienced working in psychiatric ERs in the city. Nobody was naked or screaming or obviously bleeding. The army of chairs bordering the waiting area was sparsely dotted with quietly apathetic bodies. I explained my situation to the intake coordinator, and we were quickly taken to a room, where we were met by a nurse with an inviting smile who remained positive and praised me for being vigilant as she handed me a pink cloth hospital gown, soft from repeated washings. I changed, and we were taken to a different room with an ultrasound machine.

The emergency room ultrasound experience was much different from the one that showed me my baby for the first time. The monitor was turned away from view, and the technician was stoic. She smiled when I noted that I couldn't see the screen and didn't answer when I asked why that might be. We were taken wordlessly back to our original room. I told Sam I thought something was wrong; if things were okay, they would have told us so—even though the technicians aren't supposed to. He pointed out that they aren't supposed to. I told him I hadn't heard a heartbeat. I was anxious and hoped I was overreacting. Back in the room, we waited. I am generally not a good waiter, but the amount of time that passed felt long even by the standards of people with better thresholds.

The nurse came in with the doctor, hands clasped in front of their waists after too much time had passed. It looked bad. It was bad. They told us the baby didn't have a heartbeat. They said more than that, but the white noise in my head blocked out all sounds except my heart slamming in my chest as hot tears spilled from my eyes, blurring my vision. They told me they couldn't do anything about it. I didn't understand. It was a hospital—the place where medical situations are dealt with. None of it made sense. They hugged me, told me to call my doctor in the morning, and left Sam and me crying in the hospital room.

He wanted to go. "Let's get the fuck out of here," he said. I hesitated. Something about leaving that room made it all real—like if we stayed still long enough, someone might rush in and tell us they had made a terrible mistake and everything was fine. The hospital room, with its muted pink and blue curtains around the bed, was the last place I had been before everything got worse. Exiting it felt like abandoning the version of myself that still had hope.

We eventually left. I drove home alone in my own car, ravaged by my own tears. I could not believe what was happening. My pregnancy was supposed to be a beacon of light amid the shitstorm of my dad's cancer, but it was actually just another shitstorm in the making. It was unbearable. All of it.

I've always been someone who knew things would eventually get better. Even at my saddest or sickest, I could imagine better times somewhere down the road, even if I didn't know where or how to get there. I assumed the same with the miscarriage, but it was much harder to envision. I knew there was so much horror, so much grief I would have to endure before the healing could begin, and I wanted to sleep for three months or time-jump through it all. At home, we watched TV like normal—but quieter—and I spent the night on the couch with my arm around a growing belly that would get no bigger and no longer contained a lifeforce.

****

I have not fully thought about my miscarriage in a long time. Shortly thereafter, I could easily pull the events from my memory, particularly if I had some physical reminder to tether me to what had happened. "The last time I was here, I was pregnant." "The last time I wore this shirt, I was pregnant." "That's the restaurant table we sat at when I was pregnant." I couldn't look at saltines or mashed potatoes—my short-lived pregnancy favorites—for months afterward.

Over time, the visceral recall has faded, becoming less painful, as things do. I don't casually think or talk about my miscarriage, but if I did, I would be okay. Thinking about it in the context of the story of that time in my life is different. It feels important to remember the hard parts—to be able to explain the hurt and the depression that went along with it. Miscarriages are common. I think statistically fifty percent of pregnancies end in miscarriage, but something happening often does not make it less terrible for the people going through it. Something happening often does not make it less indelible.

The hard moments in life can wear on us like a piece of glass being sandblasted. Without skills and without support, the negative circumstances become cumulative and heavy. If we don't know what we are doing, we can get trapped beneath their weight. Years later, using a rusty old key to unlock long lost memories, feelings rip me apart as if my first pregnancy loss just happened. It's a weird, unhelpful coincidence that I write this nearly eight years to the day of that miscarriage. It reminds me that the experience is always there, should I choose to torture myself—which I generally elect not to do these days. I'd rather focus on the present and the not-too-distant future instead, as they are the things I can control. My history is my history, and I wear it like a badge of honor rather than weighted shackles.

****

We went to the doctor the next morning, and she confirmed that we had lost the baby—or that the pregnancy was not viable, as the professionals say. Sitting in the same office where my pregnancy was joyfully confirmed about two months earlier was unpleasant. I could visualize the happier, naïve versions of Sam and myself sitting together on the same waiting room couch, holding hands, eager about our future. We had no idea what could potentially be reflected back at us. There was more hugging and more crying before moving on to the practicalities. We talked about next steps, none of which were good. I could wait and schedule a D&C, a surgical procedure that required anesthesia so doctors could scrape my uterine lining clean and that also came with a risk of permanent injury that could prevent future pregnancies. It also meant continuing to house a deceased fetus in my body until there was an opening on the surgical calendar; I did not like the sound of any part of it. The other option was to get a prescription pill that

I could take at home with the goal of expediting the miscarriage process. It could be done that evening.

I opted for the pill, and the doctor "described" what would happen. I'd have to insert the medication into my vagina and wait. I would bleed, and if I was not heavily bleeding by a certain point, there was another pill. It sounded about as fine as anything could in my situation. We left the office and had breakfast at one of my favorite places in town—one I would never return to because of the associations from that day—while we waited for the prescription to be filled. We went to the pet store and bought a fish. I called it my miscarriage fish until Sam initiated I give her a proper, less terrible sounding name.

That night, I followed the doctor's instructions and inserted one pill, then waited. I researched the medication. It was originally developed for another purpose but had miscarriage as an awful side effect. I thought of how terrible it must have been for all the people involved in the discovery process—one tragic opportunity growing from many others.

It didn't take long to notice what was happening in my body. It felt like a small animal—let's say a guinea pig—was placed inside my abdomen and was attempting to claw its way out, gently at first, then with the increasing intensity of something that realized it was trapped. That guinea pig was an old friend I spent a couple of days with once a month for the past twenty years—my period—and I was not happy to see him again on my couch that cool, damp October evening. I was halfway through a takeout sushi dinner— my choice, because the one with the dead baby in her gets to choose dinner—before the pain became so unbearable I needed to retreat to the couch and curl my knees beneath my chin.

I felt a warm gush between my legs when the bleeding started. There was so much blood—a terrifying amount that I was not prepared for. Blood pumped out of my body like residual water escaping a hose once the faucet has been turned off. The doctor did not warn me about this level of pain and bleeding. I was crying. I was scared. My pads weren't thick enough to capture all the blood, and I asked Sam to go to the store for more. I was bleeding and ashamed and self-conscious. I had to change my pants.

The pain continued for hours, coming in waves. I didn't know it at the time—because I didn't know anything—but I was in labor. I was not told I would have labor contractions as part of the process. At the height of my pain, I felt like I needed to throw up and thought I was going to shit my pants. I still don't know what was happening. Maybe you do.

I went to the bathroom and sat on the toilet, bent over with my head pulling toward the floor. My body ached so badly that the world around me whited out. I thought I was dying. I was alone, tears pouring down my face as fast as the blood was pouring out of my body, when it happened—I felt my unborn baby evacuate my body and plunk into the toilet like a quarter tossed into a wishing well. I felt it. I asked myself, "Did that just happen?" as the world around me started to come back into focus. "No," I unconvincingly reassured myself. "There's no way." I needed to know. I feel fortunate that the water in the toilet had grown so opaque from blood that I could not see the baby when I looked. Because, of course, I looked. While this story will remain with me until the day I leave this earth, I am glad that the image I sought in an attempt to confirm the worst will not.

Nobody told me about any of this. Nobody said I was going to go into labor and deliver a fetus in my bathroom. I'm not sure who the whitewashed version of events was for. Did they think they were helping? Were they so desensitized to the process that it no longer felt like a big deal? Maybe they were fortunate enough to have no personal experience with what they were describing. No matter their angle, the doctors were so worried about being delicate that they left me completely unprepared. I appreciate directness and information in my medical explanations rather than gentle vagueness. Don't spare any details. Please do spoil the ending, because witnessing it alone was horrific. Being prepared wouldn't have made the experience physically easier, but it might have made it less traumatizing. Dear doctors: please portray information accurately and completely to your patients. Then let them decide how to handle it. There are ways to be gentle without being neglectful.

I crawled back to the couch, hysterical, still bleeding, still in pain, and in denial about what had happened. I told Sam I could feel it, but he did not want to talk about it. I wondered if he didn't believe me, if I was being dramatic, if I had imagined it. I tried to convince myself otherwise—that it wasn't true. I lay quietly on the couch, staring at the TV, saying very little. The heavy bleeding continued. I felt embarrassed, as if I had done something wrong, as if the situation made me problematic.

At bedtime, my decision to sleep alone on the couch was met with no protests. The dogs stayed with me, sensing in their mammalian, lizard brains that something was wrong and I needed tending to. Once sleep found me—cheeks raw from rubbed-away tears and body broken from the evening's events—I bled through the largest cotton pad ever created: my underpants, my pants, and one of the two blankets I had laid out between me and the blue-gray microfiber couch cushions. In the morning, I quickly balled up my bedding and tucked it away in the laundry room like an older child hiding one last bedwetting incident.

The bleeding slowed over the next couple of days but did not stop for weeks—a constant reminder of loss. The doctor's appointments increased. I had to go back a couple of days later, then weekly for what seemed like forever—probably about a month— to make sure my body was healing correctly. When women are pregnant, all sorts of hormones essential to sustaining a growing baby accumulate in the bloodstream and do not immediately disappear when a pregnancy stops. Instead, they dwindle over time in small drips that must feel like some kind of water torture. There were weekly blood draws to watch the pregnancy hormone levels go down. It took my body a very long time to realize it was no longer pregnant, and while I waited, I spent much more time than I would have preferred in my OB-GYN waiting room, next to perfectly normal, undamaged pregnant women.

The waiting room was part of an office adjacent to the emergency room where the worst part of this chapter began. I can tell how sad I must have looked by the number of unprompted hand holdings and empty reassurances I received from office staff who had come to know me for the worst reasons. I appreciated their kindness and hated myself for needing it. I had not felt so small or broken in decades. I thought I had reached my personal bottom, but there were more bottoms to come.

FIVE

A funhouse mirror of your own design

The next hardest part of losing my pregnancy was sharing the sad news with all the people who had prematurely received our happy announcement. I did it mostly by text. I couldn't bear repeating the story to each person or facing the uncomfortable silences and awkward condolences from friends and family who were at a loss for words. Ironically, the times I have needed the most support in life are the moments I retreat from the very kinds of human contact I tell my patients will help them feel better—and that I know would help me. I recognize how important it is to push through the discomfort and allow people to take care of me, and I have tried to do more of that since. I hope you do, too.

I did not want to talk to my dad about losing the baby. I knew he deserved better than a text, even if it meant enduring the sense of disappointment that would ultimately echo in his voice. He did not need another confirmation that sometimes things don't work out, and I did not want to be the one to give it to him. I owed it to both of us to have that hard conversation and sit with all its implications. I called Camilla first, told her what happened, and quickly asked her opinion on handling my dad—a return to the logistics that so often comforted us, leaving little space for intense emotional reactions none of us could really handle. She tried to be supportive, but we were both so hollow at that point, and there wasn't much anyone could say. She told me my dad was napping and that she would text me when he woke up, and it seemed like the best time to share the worst news.

I called my dad, who was becoming a man of fewer words. He was the human version of a cut tulip wilting after several days in a vase when I shared an abridged version of what happened in tears. He told me it was terrible and that he was sorry. He didn't ask questions or pry for details. There was an ultimate hurt in the silence that followed. The fragile connection we both clung to was now severed. I stared out the glass sliding door in my kitchen into a gloomy fall yard of leafless trees. It may have been raining. My dad no longer had the capacity to find help in dinner reservations or objective perspectives. He was injured. He was quiet. We both were. We were also eager to get off the phone and put a period on this unreadable sentence.

My dad tried to hold on to being my dad in the miscarriage's wake. He called me more often to ask if I was okay and how I was feeling. He seemed more engaged—and that might have been the only nice thing to come out of the muck. It was one of the last few opportunities I had to feel a father's comfort.

About a month crawled by, and we both stopped talking about it. He knew Sam and I still wanted to try to have a baby. Sometimes hypothetical statements like "if I am pregnant" would come up in conversations about planning, but he never asked, and I never got into it. I was protecting him from knowing how hard it was for me to reintegrate back into normal person status. I was so sad so often, but I didn't want to make him feel worse than he already did, so I kept it to myself. I also knew that society had certain unwarranted expectations for grief timelines, and I endeavored to pretend I was as quickly back on track as others assumed I would be. I put my head down, focused on my work, and made plans with my friends. I probably should have been a little less performative and allowed myself to sit with my emotions longer. Denying how we feel does not help us move through hard times more quickly; instead, it traps us like a bug caught in a spider's web, struggling unsuccessfully to free itself and growing frantic.

I learned a lot about the importance of quality support from my pregnancy loss. Grief, for me, was like a multilayered cake, each tier representing a different kind of struggle—emotional, physical, mental. I also had to endure the trauma of facing all the tiers simultaneously. Each bite felt heavy, like I was swallowing something I couldn't digest. My pain lasted longer than Sam's or my support network's because it happened to me. Nobody else had to carry the physical experience or hold the detailed memories of what it was like to go through it.

Some people in my life were too uncomfortable to talk about what happened, while others overrelated and owned the story. Neither was particularly useful—I either got nothing or had to hear other tragic stories, which only made me feel more helpless. Terrible things were common and inevitable. Whether they understood or not, people instinctively cocked their heads to the side and looked at me as if I were a delicately blown glass vase that could shatter at any second. That pity head tilt, with flattened, faintly smiling lips—it's automatic, meant to signal caretaking and an attempt at empathy. But I didn't want to be on the receiving end of it. It suggested I needed empathy or caretaking, and I did not want that to be true. Not for this. Some of my friends sent flowers, and I loathed those flowers as much as I loathed the ones I later got after my dad died. It wasn't the flowers' fault—they were just an easy target.

People couldn't sit with what happened to me because it forced them to reflect on their own lives. They'd ask how far along I was and do a quick mental calculation to decide if it was okay or not. Ten weeks was early, so it made sense. I'd see their faces relax just slightly, their hands wringing one another with less tension, as if some indelible line marked when something was tragic and when it was acceptable. They had found a way to assuage their feelings with logic—something I was incapable of doing in those circumstances.

As an adult, I never had too many issues that were directly my own. I had a lot of friends and a family I could depend on. I was driven, I worked hard, and I always knew the correct-sized container for leftovers. As a wife, I was the support for Sam. Whenever my own stuff arose, I dealt with it privately. I remember an early conversation with Sam when we were dating. I was at my mother's house, and something upset me. I called him to vent, and I was met with silence. I hung up feeling ungratified and confused. As someone who did not have the greatest self-esteem or the best track record in choosing romantic partners, I consoled myself with, *"He's not the person for these types of things. I guess I'll have to fill this need elsewhere."* And so I did. It never crossed my mind to find a partner who could give me what I needed. I never thought about what I deserved and did not deserve. It was fine because none of my life things ever felt really unbearable, and when they did, I had a long list of others to share them with.

Over time, I became engrossed in the idea—maybe as a self-soothing technique—that I had to be the strong one more often, but Sam would put his stuff aside and be there for me when I needed him. As if all of my effort was being stored somewhere and would be returned in some grand outpouring of love and compassion. I would get my much-deserved return on investment. I imagined him as a tragic hero who would shed his injured man suit at lightning speed and become the uber-sensitive provider I needed when the situation ultimately arose. Unfortunately, my idea was a wish.

I lacked evidence to support my theory, but I clung tightly to it because I wanted it to be true. When we were fifteen, Sam read me a poem he had written about someone he loved, and that poem was a huge part of why I fell in love with him. He shared a sensitive and compassionate part of himself with me, and I latched on to it. I never saw another poem. What unfolded in the months and years after that afternoon sitting on his bedroom floor was often the opposite of a communicative man tuned to his feelings. I held on to that poem day after day, convinced that the sweet fifteen-year-old I met was still in there, even if he did not know how to access him.

I held out hope that my love and support would reignite in Sam a part of himself he had lost. It was how I made sense of our marriage and persevered in a relationship that sometimes felt like putting on a wool sweater that had accidentally gone through the dryer on high. The version of Sam I fell in love with never resurfaced, and it took two and a half decades and several tragic events to realize I had been looking at things through a funhouse mirror of my own design. I was left standing there, bleeding both physically and metaphorically, alone.

The value I garnered from my misadventures in partner backing is this: ensure the people in your support network can *actually* support you based on what you know to be true of them, not on a hope you have. Find people who can move their messes aside temporarily to help you clean up yours. Find people who stop you from turning your discomfort into shame—people who remind you that you are not a burden rather than reinforcing the dark thoughts lurking in the back of your mind.

It's easy to get caught up in your idea of love, to be pulled out to sea by those early months and years of bliss together—before the importance of true human communication has revealed itself. While it may not be the most fun or romantic way to conceptualize a relationship, take some time to think about what loss looks like to you and what you would want from someone in your life during that time. Make sure you're using an accurate measuring stick to determine if the people in your life can give you what you need, or if you just wish they could. Our partners tell us who they are every day, through their big and little reactions, and we bear some responsibility for the consequences if we ignore what we are being shown. I know I did.

SIX

Running to and from

In the dark frost of a New York winter that crept in while it was still fall, I slowly began to physically heal. After a couple of months of torturous appointments, my body finally stopped thinking it was pregnant, and I took what joy I could amid everything that was happening—from knowing that the trips to the doctor for the saddest bloodwork were over. I still did not feel like myself and continued leaning into the things I thought would help, but I was doing them from afar, like someone looking through the wrong end of a pair of binoculars. I was small, zoomed out from the world.

Nothing felt right, and nobody understood. I went back to the yoga class I had started taking at the gym when I was pregnant and lay on the floor, sobbing. Everyone was ready for me to stop being so withdrawn and quiet. Sam secretly texted people about me being depressed but never spoke to me about it. I didn't think it was depression, but maybe it was. I walked through the world as if a skeletal hand cloaked in a thick black robe was guiding me through my days. I was grieving the loss of a distraction I craved to help make everything with my dad feel easier. I cupped the small ember of hope in my hands, protecting it from the wind, but it extinguished anyway—and then there was nothing.

My dad started actively getting sick again in the long shadow cast by my miscarriage. Maybe it was a coincidence—or heartbreak. Maybe his ember went out too. In addition to cognitive struggles, he developed tunnel vision and was less steady on his feet. He tried to stay positive—assuring everyone he would make it to Lia's college graduation, that he had visions of living until ninety-three. His already limited list of interests shrank, and he started leaving the house less. He no longer walked laps in the carpeted hallway of his apartment building or took pride in the number of trips he made around it. He slept more and complained of neuropathy, describing it as constant pins and needles in his feet. It was hard to tell whether his tumor was coming back or if the sickness and all the invasive treatments were weighing on him.

Camilla started talking about The American Brain Tumor Association, an organization that raised money for brain cancer research and was holding a 5K race at the end of November. I decided to run in the race with my family and hoped my body would cooperate. Camilla, Lia, and I created a team, solicited donations from friends and family, and made T-shirts. The race was a good distraction—another small sliver of life we could control.

We were connecting around something positive for the first time in a long while. It felt exciting to pick the right shade of pink for the shirt logos and focus on some tagline minutiae. I looked forward to checking in with Camilla in the evening to see how much money we had raised during the day. It felt like we were doing something instead of disappearing into quicksand—and it was reinvigorating.

I started running on the treadmill at the gym once my body allowed it. I was enlivened by my newly unearthed family connections, though still physically uncomfortable and deeply sad. Anyone paying attention might have thought me insane—this woman alone at the gym, crying as she ran very slowly on a treadmill. I was still so broken, so devastated by my fleeting pregnancy and the consequences of it that had taken a toll on my body, and that I was trying to train for a short race in honor of my dying father. Yuck. To all of it. So, I cried and ran and cared very little about how the world perceived me.

Manhattan was sunny and cold on race morning. The few trees dotting the Upper West Side sidewalk held out bare branches that danced in the wind rolling off the Hudson River. I met Camilla under a tent at the table adorned with our team name, "The Landes Ladies." Lia was there with school friends to support her, and Sam and my mother came for me. My dad was too sick and tired to spend a couple of hours in the elements, instead napping on the couch while we gathered for him. I cried in the arms of Camilla's friend when she asked how I was doing. That question always got me. My parts felt tied together with a string as thin as dental floss, and it all unraveled when someone asked me about me.

The race had an air of melancholy coated in happiness. Some teams were survivors who had successfully beaten different types of brain tumors, and others were families there to mourn lost loved ones. We were in the middle—brain cancer purgatory—though we knew which side we would ultimately end up on. We listened to speeches by local celebrities and foundation members trying to infuse the crowd with optimism and cheered for what we could. I hugged a stranger wearing a shirt proclaiming she had beaten cancer and run the New York City Marathon weeks earlier.

It was a big deal for me to speak to strangers, let alone touch them, but she was my god in that moment. A person who had overcome insurmountable odds, ran a marathon, and was here to help raise money for others. A woman who was not destroyed by her own story but was carving a path forward. I wanted to be her. I realized at that moment that I wasn't just running for my dad—I was running for my lost baby and for the family I did not want to lose. I was running to reclaim the part of me that was drowning in grief and unanswered questions.

I was the only one from my team to run in the race, and I did so in one of my dad's tennis shirts. I stepped from the starting line like a person new to her own body and unfamiliar with its engineering. I cried as I ran. It was cathartic and terrible—the kind of necessary release that does not feel better on the other side. There is a photograph of me captured during the race; I had noticed someone from our group on the sidelines and, conjuring a smile, raised my fists over my head—a gesture that usually signals optimism and victory. Running alone in a brain cancer race was not innately joyful, but it did mark the beginning of my efforts to start exiting the black cloud that had flooded my brain since the miscarriage. I'm not sure if the pose was for me or for a photographer I was trying to convince that I was happy to be competing in a brain cancer race—a calendar page turn away from a miscarriage.

After the race, I tried to live as normally as possible. I made plans for the holidays and shopped for gifts. I focused on a New Year's Day brunch I had organized with some of my childhood friends while I was still pregnant. Once I resumed talking about the gathering, my best friend Fiona asked, "Are you sure you want to do this?" and I affirmed that I did. It wasn't the party she was worried about, but the context of the party, which would be attended by Sarah, another one of my very close friends who was also pregnant. Sarah, whom I had known since kindergarten and who was ultimately my favorite college roommate, had also struggled with fertility—only getting pregnant about six months before I did. We hadn't spoken much since she announced her good news, and I had not gotten around to telling her that I was pregnant during the short time that I was. It didn't make sense to tell her my story after the fact, as if talking about my miscarriage would have some direct impact on the outcome of her pregnancy. I did not want to worry her, so I said nothing.

Fiona was right, as she often is; the brunch was much harder than I thought. I feigned happiness and pretended nothing was wrong. I tried not to think about how nice it would have been to share pregnancy stories at that brunch, to compare growing bellies and complain about how our bodies were changing together. I stuffed down my brutal internal monologue of how disappointing it would be not to have children of the same age growing up together with elaborately crafted deviled eggs and brie-filled puff pastry cups. When I could no longer maintain the veneer, I excused myself to cry alone in the same bathroom where I miscarried. It was excruciating—a pointed reminder of how far I was from the people I called closest.

My tactic of leaning into others and distracting myself with plans was not working after my miscarriage and my dad's decompensation. I held myself back from pushing my internal annihilation button, a skill that I developed in my mid-twenties and was appreciative of in my early thirties. I grew to learn that the nights I wanted to drink too much or be reckless were probably the nights I should stay home to avoid problems. When I was younger, I used running as self-destructive behavior masked in a socially acceptable activity. I would get upset, go for a run, ignore the signs my body gave me to stop or slow down, and would continue until I threw up or had a migraine and was too exhausted to think of anything else. It was just as numbing and counterproductive as drinking too much.

The winter after my miscarriage was full of disappointment and sorrow, but by early spring I was ready to pull from my pocket some of what I took away from the brain cancer race—that I could connect to others through shared experiences, that I had something to offer, that I could feel proud and in control. In the hours following the run, my mental state transformed from an Alaskan deep-sea fishing boat being violently overtaken by black glacial waves crashing over it to a raft softly bobbing in the warm turquoise Caribbean Sea. It was good. Not just distract yourself from the bad good, but actually good. I craved the internal calm. I chose to focus on what worked and began running regularly. Starting was a humbling endeavor that left me achy, winded, and very aware that I was not fast. I kept at it and felt better as the weeks went on and I was able to see my times decrease and my endurance increase—signs of progress.

I started running outside before the cold relented long enough for the ground to thaw. I lived on a winding, hilly dirt road interconnected with similar roads like a rural subway map—a perfect place to escape without too much worry about cars or pedestrians. Sometimes I'd wave to someone on horseback. The terrain was not easy, but it was beautiful—roads lined with umbrellas of trees that opened up around curves to expansive mountain views glowing like flames as the sun sank beneath the earth. It was silent out there, save for the caws of hawks overhead and distant animals breaking twigs as they pranced through the forest brush. In the quiet, there was nothing—and that nothing was beautiful.

On my woodland runs, I let down my guard, turned off the outside world, and sank into myself in a way that felt so warm and so comforting. Running became my break from everything. I shut out my dad, shut out my sadness, and focused solely on myself— the thuds of my footsteps over my headphones and the rasps of my breathing within my own mind. The only thing I was responsible for while running was keeping track of where I was and whether I wanted to listen to or skip the next song that popped up on my playlist. There was no cancer, no miscarriages, no tornadoes of negative feelings that those things created to worry about. With my mind cleared of its regular murkiness, I could decide who I was and what I wanted from life. On the runs, I didn't feel like crumpled-up paper. I felt like an unstoppable warrior—and that feeling was addicting.

My runs became puzzles to unlock—I could choose my roads and plot my course. It was an hour in the day when I was in control and knew exactly what was going to happen, an experience that had become an anomaly. It improved my self-efficacy—one of my favorite psychology terms to teach others. Self-efficacy is like self-esteem, but different in a very important way. It is the belief that we are capable of doing things in general and is hugely important for navigating tough times. When self-esteem screams, "I am great," self-efficacy whispers, "I can be great." It's knowing that you can figure something out, even if you haven't done it yet.

The self-efficacy I earned from running reminded me that I could be good even if I didn't feel good—that I would get through the darkness even though I had not yet found the flashlight. I knew there was a flashlight for me somewhere. In the months following the miscarriage and the return of my dad's cancer, I needed such reminders. I had something to focus on, something to motivate me, and the side effect of extra endorphins coupled with physical exhaustion at the end of it wasn't too bad. It felt like the least lethal opioid. Life still didn't feel okay, but a small crack of bright light formed in my brain, allowing me to entertain the idea that maybe, at some point, it would. I gripped that idea so tightly all my joints ached. I kept getting better and feeling better. I gained the courage to sign up for a half marathon, which I ran three months later. My dad was the first person I called when I was done to brag about my time. He garnered whatever enthusiasm he had left to tell me I did good, and he was proud of me. A year later, he would be gone.

What all of this means is: figure out whatever that focus is for you and hold on to it. Sometimes the things we give ourselves are the only things we have—the only things that remind us of who we are outside of whatever tragedy we're going through. For me, it was running. For you, it can be anything, so long as it does no harm and makes you feel like you are home. We can so easily lose ourselves in sadness, in tragedy, in loss—but we need to find a way to be our own lifelines. Do what it takes to find your self-efficacy. Learn Latin, lift weights, climb stairs, cook extravagant French meals, do crafts, do a comparative analysis of every pizza place in your area, rescue animals. Whatever it is, make it yours. Hold on to it as if your life depends on it—because honestly, during the worst times, it does.

SEVEN

Choosing which battles to choose

The next year moved like a boulder on a downhill roll. Time was punctuated by my dad's doctor's appointments, brain scans, and failed attempts at getting pregnant again. My dad was getting worse; he was walking into things and falling without any external influence. I'd meet him for dinner, and each meal was full of risks lurking within every cracked sidewalk or uneven curb. We started eating out closer to his house or ordering in. If he knew what was happening, he never talked about it. I wonder if he was scared—or if the part of his brain that would have let him feel scared had atrophied to the point of an absence of self-awareness. I hope that was the case. I hope his internal experience was easier than mine, but I somehow doubt it.

He started forgetting more things—common things he knew and talked about all the time. The highlight of his long stints inside MRI tubes was that they let him pick the music. He always chose Bruce Springsteen, requesting it with a nodding smile and an elongated "Bruuuuuuce," spoken in a rasped voice an octave lower than his usual. As he got worse, he couldn't remember Bruce Springsteen's name. He'd rehearse it in the waiting room as we sat together. "Who's the guy I like?" he'd repeatedly ask, and I answered him with a soft grin that must have seemed tinged with dejection to onlookers every time.

Gwenn and her family came to see my dad in December. We scheduled family meals and tried to pretend they would be as they historically were. Nearly three months out from my miscarriage, I still felt like I was plastering on my functional human mask whenever I left the house and had to engage with others.

We went to brunch one morning, and it rained a cold winter rain as we left the restaurant. All the adults forgot what to do. We stood under an awning for too long, waiting for the rain to stop, arguing over why nobody thought to bring an umbrella. Everyone complained as my dad and I stood quietly next to each other. He turned to me and, out of nowhere, asked if I was getting divorced. The question shook me. It wasn't something I had considered, and I wasn't sure why he had. It was a strange thing for my dad—who did not seem aware of very much these days—to ask me in the absence of any contextual cues. I guess there were contextual cues. It was a very serious question for a man who had become averse to serious questions since he got sick.

My dad's query was particularly unsettling because he knew things. There were certain things he had seen over the years that had a clairvoyant quality to them. I never believed in ghosts or fortune telling, but I did believe in my dad's visions and had witnessed them. When I was three, we woke up on Easter Sunday—a holiday my Jewish family did not celebrate—to find that my dad's car had been stolen from our driveway.

After making all the necessary phone calls and filing the reports, we went to breakfast at our favorite local diner in my mother's car. Amid eating in our brown pleather booth, my dad popped his head up from his egg white omelet and told my mother he knew where the car was. She was skeptical, asking the kinds of questions a rational person would ask of someone who had just made a seemingly irrational statement: "How do you know where the car is? Why would the car be there?" My dad had no answers, reiterating that he knew where the car was—Flushing Meadows Park.

We had never been to the iconic Queens Park as a family, nor had my parents spent time there alone. Not only did my dad know that the car was in the park, but he said, in that diner that Easter morning, that he knew exactly where it was. My mom still doubted him but humored him with a drive. I remember them chatting in the car and how the talking diminished as we pulled up to the area my dad directed us to—his light coffee-brown Toyota Celica sat there, just as he said it would. He had no idea how he knew the car was there, but he saw it in his mind somehow. The story became a family legend, told to mostly skeptical audiences over the years.

Another time when my dad displayed an astonishing level of intuitiveness was related to me and Sam. Sam and I began dating when we were sophomores in high school. As we got to know one another, I learned that he had attended the elementary school where my dad worked, and my dad was his computer teacher. Sam remembered my dad as a stern man; he probably added that my dad was a dick who always sent him on errands. It was a crazy coincidence. I was attending a high school out of district, and Sam had moved from a completely different part of Queens to my high school's district—the chances that we would meet one another, let alone that he would know my dad, seemed so slim.

My high school was massive. Our senior class had 1,000 students, and the graduation ceremony took place at Nassau Coliseum, a Long

Island arena for professional hockey games and big-ticket musicians. Sam and I did not have classes together and met at a one-time random assembly because he was sitting next to a friend of his who liked me and kept leaning forward to tug my hair. I only saw the boy I would marry over a decade later when I turned around to yell at the friend and get him to stop pestering me. So many random acts had to align for us.

I remember going home and telling my dad that my boyfriend knew him. I told him Sam's name and watched the color drain from my dad's face. I worried that he was mad at me for something, which was, and continues to be my automatic assumption in situations where I sense that someone is displeased. He assured me that nothing was wrong, that he liked my boyfriend as a child. He remembered sending him on errands and said he did so because Sam was one of the good, smart kids he knew would make it back to the classroom.

Later, I asked my mom why my dad seemed so upset, and she explained that he had a vision of Sam and me getting married when he knew Sam as a quiet ten-year-old child from a completely different world. I assumed our being together was some kind of premonition. Maybe it was. Maybe that's what kept bringing us back to one another over the years, as the ocean that is life moved us in all sorts of directions.

So when my dad asked me randomly, under a gray rainy sky protected by an awning, if Sam and I were getting divorced, I wondered if he knew something he wasn't saying. Maybe. Maybe he saw how sad I was and picked up on my attending most recent family gatherings alone. Maybe he just knew it. My marriage did indeed feel like it was falling apart. I hadn't rebounded from the miscarriage, and I didn't feel we grew from it as a couple. And then there was this extended cancer tragedy. We ignored the serious things, replacing deep conversations with unspeaking car rides to the gym, where we mostly worked out separately. Sam didn't—or couldn't—step up. He was waiting me out. I was waiting for more. Neither of us got what we wanted.

I thought about the conversation with my dad on my long, dreary train ride home. I was unsettled by his words for unknown reasons, like they triggered some internal itch I was unable to scratch. When I got home, I found Sam in the living room and told him what my dad had said, hoping for some reassurance that the question was purely brain cancer–fueled. I envisioned him being astonished, stepping toward me with wide eyes and a smile, proclaiming, *"What? That's crazy! I love you, and I'm not going anywhere!"* before giving me a full-body hug and kissing my head.

The reaction I received was more in line with what the factual part of my brain knew of Sam and less in line with what the emotional side yearned for. He looked at me and said, "Okay." *Okay?* I asked him what he thought my dad was picking up on, and he said, "Nothing." *Nothing?* Why didn't what I was telling him bother him? It felt huge and ominous that a person who had spent years as an observer of our marriage was detecting cracks we did not see—brain cancer or not.

Sam did not seem fazed by the suggestion of the dissolution of our relationship; he did not think it was a premonition. He went back to sawing wood for a staircase he was building, and we went on as we had been—barreling down a tunnel neither of us wanted to be in.

I made a decision to let go of my father's premonition and focus on the present. I wanted to enjoy the rest of my visit with Gwenn and my family. I was hungry for closeness; however, I was reminded of the gaps that existed between Gwenn and me and our perception of my dad during that December visit. It felt reminiscent of the situation ten years earlier when my dad separately told us that Camilla was pregnant.

Gwenn and I went out to dinner with my dad at the end of her December trip to New York. I don't remember who was there. I don't remember where we went. When we left—wherever we were, with whomever came with us—my dad walked, with his now-familiar wobbly stride, toward the curb of a Manhattan sidewalk dressed in darkness and wind. Gwenn reached for his hand as we exited the restaurant. It was a logical move: hold the hand of the unbalanced man to help steady him, to keep him safe and free from further injury. But my dad, who was no longer capable of remaining in a logical space, swatted Gwenn's hand away as if she were a pickpocket he'd caught attempting to lift his wallet. She tried to reason with him, explaining that she thought he would fall. But he yelled, "Get away from me," and continued on his way.

As I watched the interaction, I saw the hurt and rejection wash over Gwenn's face before she turned her attention—and frustration—to me. She wanted me to fight with my dad for his hand too, and I refused. She was upset with me, upset with him, upset with all of it. She asked what we would do if he fell, and I told her we would pick him up.

Gwenn did not find comfort in my response, and I can see how my words could have been interpreted as cavalier—as minimizing a grave situation. It was neither of those things. I knew it would be awful for my dad to fall, maybe even catastrophic, but I also recognized how infantilizing it must have felt for him to be viewed as someone who could not walk off a curb by himself—even though he was, in fact, someone who could not be trusted to safely walk off a curb by himself.

I decided to prioritize my dad's emotional needs and deal with whatever came next. Insisting he do something that was, in actuality, a really good idea wasn't worth his resentment. My dad's weight in the argument felt bigger than the situation—like more was at stake than just his skin and bones. His dignity. Our relationship. I was looking at the bigger picture. How we would relate to one another in the coming months seemed more relevant to me, and I chose to focus on those goals, as I had done with him many years ago. In the long term, the bad idea may be the better idea.

I can relate a thematically similar professional tale to highlight the importance of choosing one's battles. At the forensic psychiatric hospital, I worked with a man who, decades ago, had done a very illegal and very societally frowned-upon thing with his child. At the time, he acted on the belief that doing that thing was his destiny. This belief was reinforced by the voices and thoughts in his head—a feature of serious psychiatric diagnoses—and was probably maintained, in part, by the subconscious desire to avoid discomfort of realizing that he had done something terrible for no reason at all. He held steadfast to his beliefs, and his insistence that he had done nothing wrong resulted in him being disliked by staff and other patients. Clinicians would challenge him, trying to poke holes in his concrete perspective, but he would dig in further and ultimately stop talking.

My patient spent over twenty years of his life trying to convince others not to hate him but was continually met with people trying to convince him that he had done something awful. It was not very therapeutic, and it always seemed to end with him making threats about God's wrath. At some point, after engaging in many circular conversations with him about laws and morals, I decided to stop. When he'd meet with me or with the team, he would start his diatribe about all his justifications, and I cut it off. "Let's agree to disagree," I'd say.

At first, my response disarmed him. He was used to fighting and was unsure how to relate without it. Eventually, he let his guard down, and we were able to talk about other things—his childhood, who he was as a teenager and a young adult. We spoke about the time in his life before his brain defied him and his symptoms began. His hostility eased, and with it came a willingness to listen to me about other things, like unit rules. He came to me when he needed help. We formed a relationship that circumvented the seemingly unchanging beliefs that kept him involuntarily hospitalized. My approach did not achieve the overarching goal of getting him out of the hospital, but it did make our time together more pleasant.

While the similarities between my patient and my father begin and end with this connection, I used the same logic to navigate strong-willed ideas. When dealing with the people in your life—whether they are psychotic, have brain cancer, some other issue, or no issues at all—think of a long-term goal and hold on to it. Then measure all your short-term interactions against it and ensure they are in line.

With my patient and with my father, I pushed glaring logic out of the way to meet my goal of having as positive and supportive a relationship as possible. There was no convincing either of them about what should or should not be, so I found ways to work around it. You can do this too. If your overall goal is to have a nice relationship with your sister, then maybe that offhand comment about her weight, hairstyle, or political affiliation will seem less worth it. Choose your battles and agree to disagree when it makes sense to do so.

EIGHT

Because I'm sad

My dad began to fall more often as the tumor in his brain continued to displace his healthy white matter. About thirty months post-surgery, the magic of his clinical trial drugs appeared to be fading. The first time I saw him fall was at Rue 57, a French restaurant in Midtown during a dinner with my nieces, my brother-in-law Ted, and Gwenn. The restaurant, located by Central Park East, had become one of my dad's favorites. It was the place I had eaten with my dad and Camilla many months earlier when I was pregnant, and something still felt right. I had not been back to the restaurant since my happier times and had not wanted to go back. I shrank into myself more and more as we walked closer. Maybe I was dissociating. Nobody knew how I felt. I had an audio recording of my own voice saying "keep it together" playing on a perpetual loop in my brain, and it was all I could hear by the time we were waiting in the loud, crowded vestibule for our reservation.

We were seated at a large round table cloaked in a white tablecloth, adorned with a stack of plates barricaded on each side by a small army of forks and knives at each place setting. Once we had all settled in and unfurled our napkins, my dad decided it was too loud and too crowded. I felt my anxiety rise through my stomach and into my limbs as he asked to switch to a different table; this had become a thing, and I was unsure if it was related to his cancer or just a byproduct of old age. It was common for this new version of my dad to decide a particular restaurant table was unacceptable far too late in the seating process, and I was bothered by it on multiple levels.

I have realized that I am overaccommodating, so the thought of inconveniencing the restaurant staff always felt huge to me, particularly at 7:00 p.m. on a Saturday. It would have taken a dead rat falling from the ceiling into my lap for me to complain in a restaurant, and the distaste for a particular table certainly did not rise to the necessary threshold. I was uncomfortable with the theatrics of it all—the nearby patrons all looking at the table of people who had just sat down, maybe ate some bread, and were now getting up to move elsewhere. I wouldn't have enjoyed any of it during normal times, but post–cancer diagnosis, it felt awful, like we were riding on a parade float beneath an illuminated sign flashing, "We are unwell! Please spend your meal guessing why and how!"

My internal discomfort aside, the man with terminal cancer gets to steer the ship, so I smiled in a way that I hoped communicated, "I am so sorry," as my dad requested to be seated in a new location. The staff obliged, and we were directed to a table downstairs— down a spiral marble staircase, of course. To add another layer to the meal that was beginning to feel like an Indiana Jones puzzle, my dad was wearing his brown suede clunky winter boots that looked as if they were plucked from a child's drawing. By pure design, the boots were not capable of navigating a spiral staircase, let alone when worn in a size too large by a man with brain damage.

My dad managed not to fall walking to the new table, inexplicably and to my great relief. I perked up again—starting to smile and joke with my nieces—when, with no warning at all, he fell backward out of his chair, crashing to the ground and landing like an overturned tortoise. A sea of people turned to our table, mouths gaping. I'm not sure if the world went silent or if my brain shut out all the noises.

A couple of waiters rushed to the table and assisted Ted in hoisting my dad back into place. He glared when we asked if he was okay—like we were wrong for checking whether he had hit his head on a tile floor—and murmured that he was fine. My dad settled into silence for the remainder of the meal. I wanted to pretend that everything was fine, for my nieces and for myself, but I couldn't.

I stared at the white ceramic bread dish on the table in front of me with disbelief, barely catching the muffled voices of the rest of our party ordering their dinners. I battled to keep the stinging tears pooling in my lower eyelids from spilling over my face. I did not want to cry. I did not want to let on that I knew something truly bad had just happened. I did not want to invite the dreaded "Are you okay?" from anyone, which would have sent me into an emotional tailspin.

Did that actually just happen? Is this where we're at? The fall was embarrassing and worrisome, but people fall. Earlier that week, I had slipped on the ice-glazed snow in my yard and slid down a small hill on my butt one early morning while letting my dogs out. The part I honed in on was how he couldn't get up afterward. The doctors warned of increasing cognitive and motor issues as his cancer progressed, and his falling and being unable to get up on his own signaled that the dinner incident was not an anomaly—that there were more bad falls to come. I worried that the time the clinical trials had gifted us was running out and that we would start barreling downward at an accelerated pace.

Camilla and I tried to pretend that things were going to be okay—until we couldn't. My dad, who rollerbladed, coached tennis, and exercised, was no longer safe to go outside alone. He was falling too often. He needed too much help. He wasn't ready to admit that his most basic adult autonomy was being taken away, so we orchestrated a fantasy around him for a while. We came up with reasons to spend time together and not go places, and we were very intentional in choosing where we did go—somewhere close, with no stairs, that would not be very crowded and would be easy to leave if something bad happened.

Camilla and Lia went to Boston one weekend for a much-needed break from the stress and rough seas, and I volunteered to care for my dad, who did not think he needed caretaking. He didn't want me to sleep over but relented when I insisted that I was doing it because it was easier for me, not because I was trying to monitor him. Consistent with who he was, I could stay at his apartment if it meant he was helping me—not if I was trying to take care of him.

I knew he was going to want to eat out somewhere. He still wanted to be in the world he used to know. Every encounter was a subconscious attempt to recreate what he had lost—dinners where he got to be the dad taking care of his daughter and running the show. I did not want to take the opportunity for validation from him, and I also knew that I was not capable of managing him outside the confines of a carpeted space with low-to-the-ground furniture should anything go wrong.

We spoke on the phone in the days leading up to the weekend, and I casually suggested that we stay in and I cook him dinner, as

I had done when he first left my mother and moved into his own apartment. I expected pushback but unexpectedly received a happy "sure, that would be great" in return. I quickly ordered groceries to be delivered to his apartment upon my arrival, so there would be no room to change the plans nor for in-person supermarket outings.

I came into the city, spent time with him, went for a run shoulder to shoulder with the Hudson River and its blue sky covering while he napped, then cooked him chicken parm and roasted cauliflower—my go-to "let me cook something simple and delicious for you" meal. We ate a happy dinner together, and it felt comfortable in ways that had grown unfamiliar. There was space for genuine conversation, removed from a restaurant where the external stimuli and his internal struggles rendered him silent. We chatted casually and openly about our lives in a way that we had not done in years.

After dinner, we watched TV together on the gray living room couch, and I jabbered about whatever show was on. We ended with a late-night talk show, and when I commented that I liked the musical guest, he rewound the episode so I could watch the performance a second time—his way of giving me something when he did not have much to give. I felt at peace when I closed my eyes in Lia's unoccupied pink sparkly child's room. My dad had not gotten injured, we had not argued, and we both remembered all our lines, acting in the normal life performance we put on for one another that evening. I hoped that the energy from the night before would carry into the next.

Sam was to meet us in the city and join us for dinner the next day. I told my dad I was happy to cook again. Maybe we could all watch a movie. "NO!" he countered. "I want to take you out."

We could not convince him otherwise. Maybe it was his way of repaying me for cooking for him; maybe he felt more comfortable going to a restaurant with Sam there to physically help him if he needed it; maybe he was just sick, stubborn, and stir-crazy. Either way, we relented.

I chose a small Thai restaurant a short cab ride from his apartment that would not be crowded. I thought I planned as best I could, but I had not realized it was raining until we were stepping out of my dad's apartment building lobby. My dad insisted on sitting in the front passenger seat of the cab, with Sam and me in the back as we quietly listened to the windshield wipers skip across the window like an unwilling dog being pulled on a walk, and the gurgle of wet tires clinging to and releasing from the wet road. I watched the red, yellow, green, and white streetlights reflect back to me in a blur from the shiny puddles forming on the black asphalt.

A river flowed between the taxi and the curb as my dad attempted to step onto the sidewalk in front of the restaurant, and his foot landed in the inches-deep cold water. I received a stern look through raging eyes that would have only been deserved if I were the one who soaked his foot.

Inside, we waited for our table at the small mahogany-red bar still outlined by multicolored Christmas lights left on from the month before. My dad had started doing this thing where he would wordlessly wander off from whomever he was with, and he did so at the restaurant, presumably to dry his waterlogged sock and shoe. He did not answer when I asked where he was going, so Sam trailed him.

My dad continued to look angry when he was ultimately corralled back to the table where we were to be seated. "I had to go to the bathroom," he snapped through outraged eyes. I held my breath as he lowered his now awkward body into a small wooden chair that did not appear promising in its ability to help him maintain his balance. Once seated, he searched for his glasses in his pockets and the large backpack that he now insisted on taking everywhere but could not find them.

His vision had been failing him more in recent weeks, and I offered to read him the menu, which he refused. He was confused and disoriented. He knew it, and he made it clear that he was not happy about it. I strained to remain patient. I had been hungry when we left his apartment, but the feeling dissipated as my worry filled my stomach with acid. Somehow, we ordered, and he growled, "Well, this was a terrible idea," in the silence that filled the space previously occupied by waitstaff inquiries.

He was right—it was a terrible idea. A terrible idea as easily avoidable as it was predictable. We made it through the meal, and by the time we delivered him back to his apartment, he was exhausted, ready to sleep, ready to be alone. The flame that had been lit by our intimate dinner at home the previous night was quickly extinguished by our outing to the restaurant. It was the last meal I had with my father when he was close to lucid.

I saw my dad again in mid-January for his next round of infusion treatments and MRI results. The news shared by the doctors was not positive—and not surprising. His tumor was growing again, and the new flares were inoperable because of their location. There was nothing left to do: no surgery, no experimental treatments. We had exhausted all my dad's scientific options. I knew it had been coming, and I still couldn't believe it. I did not want it to be true.

I didn't want to cry in the office. I didn't want the moment to be about me, but I couldn't stop my eyes from welling up and my face from turning red. I sucked my lips between my teeth, as if doing so would vacuum up my emotions. I can still hear my dad saying "okay" when he got the news—the word dripping out of his mouth slowly and intentionally, as if he was leaving room for interjections that never came. It was the first time his voice had a sense of defeat, of sadness, since he first received his diagnosis. He asked what came next and was told the gentlest, most medically appropriate "nothing." He knew what it all meant. The end.

The doctors who had come to know him—and our family— were grieving too. I felt the tragedy and failure in their voices as well. I wondered how they could spend their days like this and who they cried to at night. We were all so decayed.

As the doctor talked to Camilla about a very narrow window of options, I stared at the black-and-white image of my dad's brain and the egg-sized mass within that was consuming his life force, trying to understand what had happened. I mouthed "thank you" to the doctor as we left the office, my voice trapped with a cry I was battling to keep in my throat. Camilla stayed behind to schedule more appointments as my dad and I headed past the department lobby into the stone vestibule to wait for the elevator.

The waiting area looked and sounded like a white, sterile beehive. We stood still amid the humming, organized chaos as people who were probably not in the terminal phase of cancer whizzed by us. I felt sick. I struggled to slow my thoughts, to calm myself. I had logically known our long, winding river would aggressively deposit us at this point, but the emotional impact was beyond what I could have understood. I was unable to distract myself from how I was feeling at that moment, and I cried—for the first time in this three-year ordeal—in front of my dad. I couldn't help it.

He noticed me and placed his arm around my shoulder. "Why are you crying?" he asked gently. I looked up at my gray-haired father, whose head towered nearly a foot above mine, and told him, "Because I'm sad," as I wept. We missed the elevator as he hugged me, and I cried in his arms. Around us, people came and went, like life itself.

****

The scene of my dad hugging me as I sobbed is a reel I can readily cue in my mind to this day. I will never forget that moment. It is on the list of memories of my dad's sickness that still make me cry. I am crying now as I sit at my small home office desk nearly a decade later, staring into his photographed eyes in a frame on my desk.

Back then, it felt almost good to stop forcing myself away from feeling and just be in my natural state—a sad mess of a human who had lost so much and convinced myself I had no right to be upset. I wanted my dad to know I was sad that he was sick, sad that he would be gone, and I would not know what to do. I also felt guilty for letting on that the situation was dire, for being the one who could no longer play along with my dad's positive world. I felt terrible for taking that from him, for reflecting a reality he had spent over two years evading. I was comforted by my father's all-encompassing tight hug and felt ashamed that the man who was dying was trying to make me feel better about it all when I should have been the one doing that for him.

In retrospect, what I can say is that the human emotions related to grief are complicated and painful. They create spaces within us that feel both hot and cold at the same time. I don't recommend any of it. Despite all I have learned, I still dread being inevitably placed in a similar rat's maze of loss again.

The jagged gorge between who my dad was and who he became after he got sick grew larger after that bombshell was dropped on us, fraying the small thread of hope we had clung to. He became more irritable, more often. He spoke less, and when he did, it was to communicate a need rather than to connect with another person. He grew more sensitive to sound and tone and started yelling at Lia for doing normal kid things like laughing and running around. He began fixating on certain topics, endlessly speaking about his concerns over world population and the number of children I should have—forgetting that I was starting out in the negative column. He became more resistant to changing his clothes or diverging from his sick-guy uniform. He lost interest in food in general, and specifically in food diversity.

He developed a rigid routine related to Subway sandwiches, surely the most endearing of my dad's end-of-life quirks. He wanted only one kind of sandwich—every day, for both lunch and dinner. Camilla would go to the Subway franchise near the apartment and order three identical footlong turkey sandwiches that my dad rationed for six meals, at which point she returned to Subway with the same order. The workers got to know the kind Upper West Side customer who ordered sandwiches in a very odd way. I wonder what they thought when my dad died and the sandwich orders ceased.

One day, I called my dad on my way to his apartment for lunch and asked if he wanted me to get something special. "No," he replied. When I pressed, suggesting he indulge in something he used to enjoy, he snapped back, "I already have my lunch. You do whatever you want." He was wordlessly eating half his sandwich when I arrived with my falafel.

In between the remaining gruff visits and quiet lunches, there were occasions when my dad tried to talk to me about serious issues. He would typically wait until he retired to the guest room that had become his bedroom because of the erratic hours he now kept, then muster whatever strength was left in his voice to ask me to come sit with him. My dad and I had not talked about his dying once since he got sick.

Prior to the cancer, there were instances when hypothetical conversations would arise in which he insisted he wanted to go quickly, that he did not want to suffer, and that he did not want to be kept alive. Speaking about death with a healthy dad made me uncomfortable, and I would joke, with the awkwardness of someone who did not know a real thing to say, "Don't worry, Dad, I'll smother you with a pillow when the time comes," and the conversation would stop. I was afraid of loss and its true implications years before I faced it. I made dark, quirky comments and brushed it off. When he was well, the thought of him dying— or anyone I loved dying—seemed insane and completely irrational.

Once, during a lucid moment bookended by naps, he called me into his room and told me he was leaving me something. The statement made me uncomfortable, and I tried to run from it. I didn't care about my dad's stuff or his money. I wanted my dad— not some remnants of him. I didn't want to think about what would happen after he died, because it meant actually thinking about him dying. When he was sick, I never once thought about what would become of his personal effects or finances when he was gone. I couldn't understand how some people focused so heavily on such things during times of loss. When he brought it up, I quickly shut the conversation down to reassure him that it wasn't important to me—that he was important to me. In the moment, I failed to recognize that it was important to him. He was telling me he knew he was dying and wanted to make sure I understood his wishes.

I didn't listen to my dad when he spoke about his worldly possessions. I heard his words and brushed past them. I thought I was reassuring him that he wasn't dying, but maybe he knew he was—and wanted to face it. Maybe I knew he was dying and wasn't ready to do the same. I wish I had listened to him. I wish I had given him that last moment of feeling like he was taking care of me, doing what he could to protect me. He wanted me to know that, in the midst of his sickness and whatever it was doing to him physically and mentally, he still cared for me and was concerned about what would happen when he was gone.

So the advice I give to you—and that I will take myself when I ultimately face a similar situation—is this: listen. Put your complicated feelings and wants aside to hear the words of the person who may not have many more opportunities to share them.

NINE

Get out of here

After my dad's tumor returned for a finishing blow, his doctor appointments and our days shifted from a routine rhythm into an out-of-control roller coaster. We had no choice but to hang on tight as the ride sped faster and faster. There was no more comfort in the regular, no more quiet in the monotony. The new normal was blown apart, and in the aftermath, there was chaos. My dad started falling more often in his apartment and, in his last month at home, was unable to assist others in picking him up. His body was short-circuiting.

The doormen—who had known Camilla, Lia, and my dad as pleasant, generous tenants who spoke to them in passing—became deeply acquainted with his illness during frantic late-night phone calls that sent them rushing into the apartment to help lift him. I doubt their job description mentioned assisting dying men from the floor, but they did it without hesitation. I am eternally grateful for their kindness and the support they offered.

In his last month at home, my dad's obsessive conversations shifted from his usual worries about the world and how many people there were to specific, unresolved incidents from his past.

He was haunted by unsettled ghosts clinking their chains in the back of his mind. His cancer disinhibited him and rotted the wooden lid on the box where he had locked such things away.

One story he recited on a loop concerned the dissolution of his first marriage. It was upsetting—one a child wouldn't want to know about their parents. My dad had never shared the story of his first marriage with Gwenn, a product of that marriage, because he knew it would be unnecessarily painful. He had recognized, before he got sick, that recounting his version of events would do more harm than good.

When Gwenn returned to New York for one last visit, Camilla and I primed my dad not to speak about the story. We reminded him that Gwenn did not know what had happened between her parents during the early years of her life—and that he had refrained from telling her for over four decades because he didn't want her to know. He didn't want to hurt her. He agreed to stay silent, telling us the story once more to get it out of his system—like an itch he needed to scratch one final time before someone taped oven mitts to his hands. It was the first thing my dad said to Gwenn after greeting her at the apartment door. Unsurprisingly, she was overcome by it. A brief mix of hurt and anger washed over her face before she somehow changed the subject.

That incident cast a heavy shadow over what was already expected to be a difficult weekend. Gwenn was staying at a hotel near my father's apartment, and I intended to stay with her. We had made plans for a girls' night and to get our nails done after spending time with my dad—a much-needed bonding moment amid all the sadness. We ate dinner at my dad's apartment and began discussing schedules for the evening and the next day with

Camilla when my father excused himself to use the bathroom. A loud bump and a groan followed shortly afterward.

Camilla went to check on him and then called Gwenn and me into the room, her voice taut with a stress that sounded like a rubber band stretched to the point of snapping. My dad had fallen off the toilet, landing in such a way that his half-naked body was barricading the door—making him his own prisoner. He couldn't move. Camilla left Gwenn and me to tend to him while she tried to do some damage control with Lia, who was privy to everything that was happening.

Gwenn and I tried to figure out a plan. We sat on the floor outside the bathroom and made eye contact with my dad's single visible eye as it peered back at us through the thinnest gap we could create between the door and the frame. After what felt like an entire day—but was probably about twenty minutes—we got him to slowly inch his body away from the door.

He needed very specific instructions that required the utmost concentration from him and patience from us: *Shift your left foot over. Now move your arm toward the wall. Tilt your head. Shift to your left, then to your right to move back toward the toilet.*

I could not believe how calm we were. I was in awe of Gwenn— who often seemed encumbered by anxiety—as she reverted to the strong, maternal figure I had cherished when I was young. By the bathroom, she was sure of herself and in charge. I was comforted by her energy, which reassured me that we would get through my dad's struggles.

Eventually, my dad created enough space for Gwenn and me to squeeze into the bathroom. We lifted him up—one under each arm, like two bouncers kicking a drunk out of a bar at closing time—and placed him back on the toilet. It was horrifying. At that point, it was the worst thing I had witnessed. *At that point.*

I hated that my dad needed so much help and knew it was a sign of much worse things to come. I hated seeing my strong, independent father lying pantsless and helpless on a bathroom floor, the air thick with the smell of his own shit. I knew that whatever was left of him hated needing our help—hated that Gwenn and I had to see him like that.

With the imminent danger neutralized, we decided I should stay at my dad's apartment that night in case there was another incident. I slept on the couch in his living room after we had all retreated into our separate corners to process what had happened on our own. The next day, Camilla, Gwenn, Lia, and I got our nails done while my dad napped—it was as if nothing had ever happened. I went through the motions and talked about fertility medications and pregnancy hopes with my feet in a pedicure tub. Once the initial shock abated, I looked for a silver lining in what had happened in my dad's bathroom the night before. I was sure the incident would bring Gwenn and me closer, as I had been hoping. I joked that we would be forever bonded over seeing Dad's penis. She never did get my humor.

Camilla sought 24-hour care for my dad following Gwenn's visit. It had become too hard for her in the house. She couldn't keep calling the doormen when he fell. She couldn't keep subjecting Lia to the level of disorder that swirled around the falls. My dad pushed back against the idea. He did not want help from anyone, let alone a stranger. He did not trust anyone. Eventually, he relented in the way a person without options or autonomy is forced to relent and ultimately sank deeper into his illness. He started getting paranoid. He maintained his composure in front of the home health aides and would unleash his anger about their presence once out of earshot.

One night, while Sam and I were standing in line at a fast-food restaurant waiting for a thoughtless dinner, Camilla called for my help. She asked me to talk to my dad. I heard the defeated impatience in her voice as she explained that he had been yelling at the home health aide, yelling at her, yelling at Lia. He was being irrational, and she was tired of so many months of mountains to climb with him.

He sounded small and timid when she handed him the phone. He told me that he did not like the health aide assigned to him and that he believed she was stealing from him. I was surprised to hear his accusations. Camilla had vetted Iris and seemed quite fond of her. She valued the woman who came into her home, helped her with my dad, and gave her the same kind of reprieve that Lia's babysitters had provided years earlier. I also knew by that point that my dad did not have much left to steal. His possessions had been whittled down to what could fit in a backpack and a small closet, and I did not view them as the kinds of items a sixty-year-old woman with a thick, flowery Caribbean accent would covet.

My work brain kicked in, and I approached my dad like a psychiatric patient. I was trying to parse reality from delusional thoughts. If I outright shared my doubts about his accusation, he would shut down further and refuse to listen. I asked him what was missing and was glad he could not see the look of confusion and surprise that crossed my face when he told me it was his bottle of Visine. He was completely convinced that the gentle woman tasked with caring for him was willing to risk her career and her reputation over a bottle of Visine.

He insisted Iris was a Visine thief. I reminded him of all of Camilla's expensive things in the apartment, which had a much more appealing risk-reward ratio if someone was looking to steal from him. He remained unconvinced. I asked him for his evidence, and he told me, in the tone of a notorious detective who had just cracked open a serial murder case, "My Visine is missing."

As we spoke, it became apparent that he would rather believe someone was taking what was his than accept that, despite the regimented systems he had put in place for himself, his brain was deceiving him and he was misplacing things. After twenty minutes of reassurances that did not invalidate what he was thinking or feeling, he reluctantly accepted the most likely reality. He promised me that he would look for the Visine again and would ask Camilla to open one of the dozen other bottles lining his medicine cabinet like a small teal eye-relief army, should he remain unable to find it.

The Visine story is one of the tales that Lia and I tell one another when we want to laugh about something that happened when my dad was sick. Topically, delusions are funny. It is amusing to think about someone being so steadfast about something that clearly is not true. It might have been crazy, but it was innocently so. Nobody was stabbed or pushed in front of a moving train because of my dad's Visine beliefs.

It might sound callous to laugh at another person's struggles, but we aren't laughing at my dad's. We are joking about a situation with so much absurdity and pain that we would never be able to recover from it without the moments when we can smile. The few silly stories have become our code—a way of talking around the agony without mentioning it. We can bring up the Visine thief, or the Subway sandwiches, or the frayed straw cowboy hat and feel close to one another without having to rehash the trauma that remains below them. I will always find humor where I can, while fully knowing that the sickness beneath the anecdotes pulled me apart, changed who I was, and altered the trajectory of my life.

****

It was not long before my dad needed hospice care. For those of you still unacquainted, hospice is the midworld between life and death. It's where our loved ones go when we know they have more time left without the hope of improvement. It was the quietest, saddest place, with its pale green recliner chairs made of impermeable plastic and its food-chemical cleaning solution–stagnant human body smell permeating the air. It was a difficult place to be— something I would not recommend doing if you don't have to and something I would absolutely recommend doing if you do.

Hospice was a one-way hospital that tried very hard to pretend it was a joyful place. The cream walls surrounding the elevator lobbies were adorned with cork boards pinned with color calendar printouts of activities: art classes and gentle movement classes for the mobile, support groups for the families. There was soft music in the courtyard and a mural. Walking through the tiled halls was like being in a living wax museum of a cemetery. Most people do not spend much time in hospice. People at the very end often pass quickly. Not my dad. My dad resided in hospice care for over two months, which was an anomaly—one you can decide if lucky or unlucky.

By the time my dad was admitted to the facility in the Bronx, he was barely talking. He was coughing and choking when he ate and needed to drink thickened liquids to prevent beverages from spilling down his throat faster than he could handle. His motor skills and arm strength eroded substantially. Holding the remote control and pointing it in the general vicinity of the TV was a victory. He could no longer pick up a utensil and direct it toward his mouth. When he tried, the contents of his spoon dripped onto the tray below him and onto his chest—none of it passing through his searching lips. He needed to be fed.

The nurses encouraged families to participate in patient feeding, to use it as a time of connection and a gesture of love. Conceptually, I understood the value, but I was uncomfortable feeding my dad. I knew he hated it even more. Or at least the person he was before all of this started would have hated it. I imagine the healthy version of him trapped like a small frantic plastic figurine in his own anatomical snow globe, watching in horror as his life devolved out of his control—staring out helplessly as his adult daughter offered him spoons of applesauce and unsuccessfully searched for the right tone to make the ordeal feel dignified. I'm not sure if this image is accurate. Maybe I'm wrong. Maybe he could no longer contrast in the way I did. Maybe he was happy to be surrounded by a loving family in his hardest moments and did not feel tortured or infantilized. Either way, holding a plastic spoon of food to my father's dependent face and then using the spoon side to scrape up what remained around his mouth was not a comforting situation for me.

I visited my dad at least twice a week while he was in hospice, and Camilla was there every day over the next couple of months as the remainder of his life unfurled. Lia visited as often as she was comfortable, doing so until the final weeks, during which my father no longer resembled the person he used to be in any way. I could not believe we were here, that this had become our lives. My heart was broken. I was broken. I felt like my dad was trapped in a burning building, staring at me from a window with the glass blown out, searching for help that I was unable to provide. I tried to communicate "I'm sorry" through my eyes every time they met his. I was so sorry. Sorry for both of us.

At first, he was disoriented. He would wake up after a nap, forgetting where he was and what condition he was in, and try to get up. He often needed antipsychotic medication to calm his rage at not being able to walk to the bathroom. He was furious at us for telling him no. In his irrational moments, he held Camilla and me responsible for his situation, as if we were his terrorist captors. He would yell that he had to go to the bathroom and required much reassurance to stay where he was and use the already inserted catheter. I felt a part of myself dying along with him every time the dejected acceptance filled his eyes and he relented and dropped back down into his bed.

My dad stopped actively fighting against his new universe with a little time and enough medication. He slept a lot, and when he was not sleeping, he lay in bed motionlessly, staring through the television or being fed. For a while, he recognized his visitors and was happy to see them. He'd offer me a fragile nod or some brief eye contact that let me know I still mattered.

My father's pilot light blew out in May after he was inducted into the Queens College Coaches' Hall of Fame. He had spent about thirty years coaching the men's tennis team for Queens College, and it was a shock to the school community when my dad suddenly became consumed by GBM. The school thought it would be nice to do something special for him while he was still living, as the actual induction ceremony was months away and we all knew it would be long after his death.

There was a bedside ceremony where he was given a plaque. Former colleagues, students, and friends were there to show their love and support. People gave speeches and hugged him. They tried to talk to him like the man he was—their leader, mentor, and father figure—rather than the man he became. I watched adults I had known my whole life smile bravely and excuse themselves to cry softly in the hallway, a move I had become quite accustomed to over the years of his illness.

There were flowers, balloons, and snacks all wedged into the small hospital room, forming a U around my father's bed. I was surprised to see how many people and things could fit into such a compact space. Under other circumstances, it would have been a happy occasion, but in this instance it was an award given pre-posthumously, and it was sad. It was all so sad. I'd like to think that my dad appreciated being surrounded by so many kind and familiar faces celebrating his personal and career accomplishments during his last living weeks. It was the last time my dad smiled and the second-to-last time I heard him utter a sentence—something like "wrap it up" when he was ready for everyone to leave.

Visits returned to quiet after the ceremony. There were feedings and lots of sitting still in a small pale room that always felt just a little bit sticky despite how often it must have been cleaned. I never knew what to do. It was the verbal equivalent of struggling with where to put your hands while standing alone, waiting for someone outside a bar. I wondered if he could still hear me, so sometimes I talked to him. I probably should have spoken more. I'd have these moments where I'd remember a study I heard about years ago in which coma patients thrived when they were in engaging environments and faltered when they were not, and I'd talk—telling him stories about my day or the weather or the world—but it was not easy. Feedback is what makes talking to other people reinforcing, and with my dad, there was no longer feedback. I tried to imagine the responses I would have gotten from him as I spoke, but my steam often ran out quickly. I always disliked playing pretend.

Hospice visits were easier when my schedule overlapped with Camilla's. There was less pressure to figure out what was correct as the two of us chatted like we were at brunch—a conversation my dad was privy to rather than a silent part of. We had grown more comfortable with one another during my dad's sickness, and our dialogue became more personal. For the first time, I was learning about her through her. It felt good. My dad would have loved to hear it. Maybe he did. He had always pushed for her and me to have a relationship—pushed in a way that felt too much and too fast when I was nineteen, but at the end of his illness we were ready—on unfortunate terms.

My dad's breathing began to slow as the days crawled by. Each respiration stretched out like a spiral phone cord pulled too far. Each breath becoming increasingly labored. The spaces between breaths also grew longer. His breathing became the opposite of what I had been taught in yoga—that each inhalation is connected to the next like the continuous, flowing waves of the ocean. He would sharply breathe in as if startled, breathe out, and then stop breathing for what seemed like too long. Camilla and I exchanged cautious glances during the pauses, holding our own breaths as we waited to see if he would start again or not. Neither one of us was personally acquainted with the active dying process, and we innocently—or hopefully—thought it was possible for my dad to slip away quietly without anyone realizing what was happening. The universe would soon make a point of highlighting our naivety.

I took time off work and spent a whole day with my father at the beginning of June so Camilla could have a break on her birthday and try to do something—for a brief moment—that reminded her there was more to life besides suffering and hospital rooms. My dad wasn't talking or opening his eyes much, but he was still eating enough to sustain his physical existence. I was happy to sit with him so he wouldn't be alone, but I was not happy to be there. The day felt like hours spent in a doctor's waiting room when I didn't have an appointment. I hunkered down in the large leather recliner chair in his room—one he had not sat in since his first week in the Bronx—and read while he slept, feeding him and helping him drink gelatinous water from a straw when he was awake.

When it was time to leave, I explained to my dad that I was going, that I would be back, that I loved him. I couldn't have spoken for more than two minutes when he proclaimed—in the most lucid statement I had heard him utter in nearly a month—"Get out of here." I said, "Okay, I love you," with a voice stolen by the emotional equivalent of a stomach punch and left for the elevator in tears. *Get out of here.* The last words my dad would speak to me.

I felt small and broken. Being yelled at by my minimally conscious father in the midst of his slow death reinvigorated all those miscarriage feelings about being incapable of doing things correctly. On my best days, I struggled with my dad, or anyone, being upset with me, but on my best days there were usually valid reasons for his annoyance. Not this day. I obsessed over what I had done wrong or why I was so bothersome on my drive home.

I struggled through the story when I called Camilla to debrief about the day. "How did it go?" she asked in a voice that sounded both casual and overwhelmed. "Good," I responded cautiously, "except that he screamed at me to get out when I was saying goodbye." I felt ashamed to tell her. Sharing an anecdote where I was at the brunt of my dad's irrational anger made me feel guilty. I was the no-good kid fessing up about getting scolded. I irrationally expected her to ask me what I did to upset him, and she did not meet those expectations.

After a pause, she responded, "I'm so sorry, Amanda," with a softness to her tone that sounded like an apology from someone who fully understood me at that moment. "You know he didn't mean that, right?"

Logically, I knew he did not. "Yeah, I know," poured from me in an unconvincing near whisper as I tried to stifle back tears. "Your father loves you so much, and he is so proud of everything you are doing, no matter what he says." The tears steeping from my eyes traveled across my face and lodged between my ear and the phone. I managed a high-pitched "I hope so" between sobs and agreed to check in with Camilla later. She knew I was upset, and I knew she knew and was empathetic, but something about openly crying to her still felt wrong. After the call, I buried my face in a tissue, breathed deeply through the tears, and tried to focus on what I needed to do to get through the rest of the day.

I do not often think of my father's last words when I remember him, but they continue to sting when they come to mind—or when I am pulling from the depths of my brain to write a memoir about grief. With some distance, I wonder if he was angry at my presence, or if he was telling me to leave *for me*—as if, at that moment, he realized I was sitting with him in this living coffin and wanted to protect me from it. Maybe it was his last act of grace. Neither rationalization brought me much comfort. I hated how vulnerable I felt, and how I still needed so much from someone who could no longer give it. I felt guilty for how sad I was about something so relatively insignificant compared to what he was experiencing. At that moment, I despised having feelings and needs at all. Sometimes I still do.

One sunny June morning, when the blue sky was painted with the kinds of clouds that look like comfortable places to rest and look down at the world, I got a call from Camilla. My phone rang not long after I had traversed the half-mile outdoor walk from the forensic psychiatric center parking lot to my office at the back of the hospital's compound. She said my dad had slipped into critical care—the final phase of hospice, when one's vital signs begin to slow and the doctors can predict a thirty-six-hour window. We had been barreling toward this point for months, and I was still avoidant of it—and unprepared. I told Camilla that I would finish up something stupid at work, like sending an email that was certainly not life or death, and head down to the hospital. She told me to get there—that I had been there the whole time—and that he would want me there at the end.

I called my supervisor and told him that my father, who had been dying for three years, was actively dying and I needed to go. He said he understood, and when he got off the phone, he added, "Maybe things will turn around"—which was laughably incorrect. An absurd thing to say to me in my situation. I may have laughed, and I definitely shared the odd interaction with coworkers later. *Maybe things will turn around?* Not on this planet. Even the most psychiatrically decompensated patients on my unit would have abstained from making such a delusional comment. I can now see that his response was less about what I was dealing with and more about his discomfort with death—and his own new cancer diagnosis that he was just beginning to process. Everyone's life events seem to be a projective test for someone else's, and we often convey our own worries and insecurities in the moments we're trying to guide someone else. He wasn't reassuring me that my dad would be okay; he was trying to convince himself that *he* would be okay.

I made a couple of phone calls on the hour-long drive from Middletown to the Bronx and was otherwise silent. The sky resembled the sky I saw from the streets of Manhattan on September 11, though with a higher ratio of clouds—another beautiful day that altered the course of my life. The chorus of the song "Coming Down" by the Dum Dum Girls played on repeat in my mind, drowning out whatever was actually on the radio as I casually weaved through traffic.

Not much had externally changed when I got to hospice. My dad looked like the same ghost I had been spending time with— still, silent, with his hands at his sides on a white cotton blanket that draped his body from neck to toes. His eyes remained closed. It's a strange sensation, knowing something imminently awful will happen but not knowing when. Like an asteroid barreling toward Earth. Part of me wished it would come quickly so I could move on to whatever was on the other side of his passing, and part of me wanted to sit in that room watching my father forever, like an embalmed pope captured in a clear coffin beneath Vatican City.

Camilla took a moment in the hall with all the nurses whom she was now on a first-name basis with when I got there, while I sat close to my father. I meekly greeted him with a "hi Dad," to which he did not respond. I wondered what he heard, wondered if he knew how little estimated time he had left on earth. I wanted to say something, but memories of my failed attempt at a conversation days earlier restrained me. I wanted to do something important for whatever was left of him, something that I hoped would push through the wall around his consciousness and let him know that he was loved. That he would always be loved. I played Bruce Springsteen's "Born in the U.S.A." on my phone for him and held his hand. I recalled how that song sounded from the back seat of car rides during my childhood, how it was one of the remnants of his old life that he dragged into his MRI tubes. I looked at his soft face with adrenaline plucking at my leg muscles as my palm and fingers wrapped around his.

Sam came to hospice after work to support me. None of us knew what to expect. Camilla sat in a chair on the other side of my father, across from me, and we made what little plan we could. We would stay together, hunker down for the night, and Sam would leave to take care of the dogs. Camilla and I laughed about having to order from Applebee's for dinner—the only game in town and not something either of us would have typically eaten.

I was perusing a menu of fried appetizers when my dad's breathing changed. His body looked as if he had just finished climbing a mountain, his chest heaving up and down rather than lying motionlessly in bed. My dad had been given an oxygen mask at some point prior, but the nurses removed it when they saw how he was breathing. They said he would be more comfortable without it in his last moments and thought we would want to be able to see his face. Camilla and I sat beside him, each holding his hand. We took turns telling him how much we loved him, how proud we were of him for fighting, and how it was okay to let go.

As much as my dad thought he would want the end to come quickly, his body did not. His breathing became deeper and more exaggerated, like someone picking up an accordion for the first time, giving it a try, and pressing the sides together in frustration when the noises coming from it were not beautiful. His eyes opened wide, and he looked through us, presumably seeing nothing. The nurses explained that once the lungs fail to work independently, the diaphragm takes over in a final effort to push air in and out of the body to preserve life. It was fascinating to learn about and horrifying to watch. It looked like it hurt, though the nurses assured us otherwise. I wondered how they knew, having never gone through it themselves. My father was battling himself in the last seconds of his life, fighting until the end. Even as his organs shut down, he waged war.

I held my dad's hand long after he wrestled his last breath from his body and sobbed. Three years' worth of poorly contained sadness rushed out of me and over the body of my now-deceased father. His death felt as grueling as his sickness. As Dylan Thomas commanded, he did not go gentle into that good night—it was the hardest thing I've ever borne witness to. I had imagined what his death would look like, and in my mind, his end was peaceful, based on what I knew from movies and TV shows. People took their last breaths, and life left their bodies gently.

My dad's death was not peaceful or gentle. His eyes did not close when it was over, instead frozen open in a perpetual last gasp. A nurse came in and used the side of her hand to close my father's eyelids—one last act of compassion. She softly, with that head-tilted-to-the-side, pursed-lip smile I had grown to loathe, told us to take as long as we needed. I did not resent the empathy or pity in her tone. I embraced it. I knew I deserved it. I hugged Camilla, and we cried together, though even in that moment our versions of grief felt distinct.

I did not want to leave my father's room once he was gone. It seemed wrong to stroll away from what I had witnessed and what I had carried with me throughout his cancer—and continue to go about life. I realized I was not ready to see what life was like on the other side of his sickness. I wanted to stay in that room as long as I could. I felt frozen, as I had that afternoon in the ER after learning I miscarried. I breathed slowly and deeply, grateful that I could and guilty that he could not. I said my goodbyes to the nurses I would never see again as I left, and as I walked out into the mild June evening air, I heard his healthy voice in my head asking, "What are you doing?" and telling me to focus.

TEN

There are treasures beneath avalanches

My dad's slow-motion death was not the end of my hard times. My life continued to devolve for many months after the small black plastic rectangle containing his ashes was delivered to my house. His passing did not erase my ongoing struggles with fertility. I had surgery to remove a fibroid tumor from my uterus a week after he died. I underwent invasive tests that filled my uterus with saline solution, filled my fallopian tubes with dye, and one where a piece of my uterus was biopsied—all while I was awake and without any numbing agent. My rant about how doctors often incorrectly use words like "pinch" or "slight burn" to describe medical procedures typically follows my rant about the pain scale. I'll spare you the details, but I'm sure by this point you can guess my perspective.

The compounding blows took a further toll on my relationship with Sam. I wanted to resume our slow march toward pregnancy, but he was no longer willing to allow our lives to be dictated by ovulation test strips. I resented him for continuing to stand in the way of the one thing I thought would help me. It seemed like a selfish choice for someone who allegedly loved me and still wanted to build a life together. We started drifting apart—or rather, I started drifting apart—and the routines that previously felt so important to me seemed to matter less. We stopped going to bed at the same time because I wanted to stay up without considering him or his needs. The relief I found in my solitary running time was no longer enough, so I started taking more. I cared less when he went out with his friends after work and was no longer plagued by insomnia and stomach aches when his plans to have one beer degenerated into him staying out past last call and ignoring my texts about when he was coming home.

Honestly, it was nice to disengage. My twenties were plagued by worry and desperation related to our relationship, and I liked feeling the emotional heaviness lift. I liked having one less negative thing to fixate on. In the space I made, I realized that I was angry about incidents that happened decades ago and were never resolved. Nothing ever felt resolved. While we were together, our typical pattern was that something would happen—maybe related to drugs or alcohol or failed obligations—and I would get upset. I'd stay silent, always waiting for him to bring up whatever happened and apologize, always being disappointed, until my body and mind felt like a pressure cooker with a jammed release valve.

By nature, I am a talker. I have a pretty good understanding of my emotions and am comforted by putting them into words. With the right person, communicating raises awareness and rights wrongs. We learn how the other person feels about something, and, if it is reasonable to do so, we alter our behavior accordingly. With the right person, communication builds intimacy and connectedness, which are the main operating systems of thriving relationships. I was not with the right person.

My efforts to talk to Sam about whatever happened were typically met with silence or a counteraccusation that was designed to make me feel like I was the problem. I reprogrammed myself to accept that talking only made issues worse and that the best course of action was to find a way to get over it on my own and move on. The tactic was a plug that kept the dam blocked for many years. It was so efficient that I failed to realize what was building on the other side, or what it would look like when I lost my fear of the consequences and the plug disintegrated. I became that scene in *Fight Club* where Brad Pitt forces Ed Norton's character to drive with his hands off the steering wheel. When I let go, everything came out.

I assumed that revisiting all the dark times in Sam and my relationship would offer the closure I was searching for—that he would give me some explanation for why things unfolded the way they did in our youth, and I would finally be able to understand, forgive him, and move on. It didn't. I was still angry. We began fighting over small things—things I would have previously let go but couldn't anymore. Emboldened by my newfound indifference, I voiced my opinions about household decisions and stopped blindly accepting Sam's perspective. He stared at me wide-eyed the day I challenged his decision to buy more sheetrock that we needed for a home renovation project instead of the new mattress we wanted to feel more comfortable in our own space. I saw barely suppressed resentment in his pursed lips as I questioned his choice and suggested there might be a better one. He yelled at me—yelled at me for one of the first times in our marriage, "Fine. Do whatever you want." It seemed that he was angry too. Our symbiotic relationship had shifted.

The fights never seemed to have conclusions. There were empty promises about couples therapy and resisting bad habits related to vices, but no follow-through. He grew to resent me for wanting more than he could give, and I grew more bitter that my needs were not being met. It's not a very original story. We spent five months spinning around, getting further from one another with each rotation. One November night, we had a conversation in the pitch-black of our bedroom atop the mattress I had insisted we purchase, and he asked if we should get divorced. "I think so," I offered. I smiled an uncontrollable Cheshire Cat smile of relief as the words spilled from my lips. I felt happy for the first time in months, and I felt no guilt as I basked in the relief.

By December, six months after my dad's death, I found myself living alone in a rental apartment close to my job and far from the life I thought I was building for myself. Though separation and divorce were ultimately necessary, the decision was not simple, and it was not a clean break. Despite the issues that evolved over the years and then erupted, I loved Sam. We had a nice life together, and it was those good times—the vacations, the parties, the special dates—that I found myself focusing on as everything fell apart. I would miss our big holiday gatherings and the weekends planned around our friends coming to visit us. I'd miss the countertops I picked out for our house and the way the sun shone through the trees when I returned home from a run at dusk.

I was unsure in my decision to begin again at age thirty-eight. Would I ever find what I was looking for from another person? Does it even exist? I realized that the positive items my brain was diverting to were not exclusive to Sam or the connection between us. I was mourning the people, places, and things that existed outside of our core unit, things that were valuable because they felt innately special, rather than things that could only be special because he was a part of them.

Divorce is different from a breakup. Breakups are hard, but divorces have much more debris from the fallout. In a breakup, distinct friend groups can remain intact and there is much less division of property, or pets. Divorce feels like an entire garden dying at once after it was accidentally watered with bleach. Sam and I had known one another since we were fifteen and our lives were interwoven in many ways.

Though a majority of our friend group was technically his, they had been ours since we were practically children, and I shared many intimate moments with them over two decades. I hung out with them without Sam, and we had deep talks about our lives and our goals. We celebrated Thanksgivings, Christmas Eves, and New Year's in my apartment. Just as many of Sam's friends attended my dad's memorial service as my own. They had become my people. While my marriage silently eroded over the years, one minute my friends were there, and the next, they were gone. I accept that people ultimately choose sides when a marriage ends, and they made theirs—though it was a choice I never asked for. I both do and do not understand why one relationship ending must naturally sever a dozen others.

Gwenn was another loss. Seeing our dad's penis did not bring us closer—as I had hoped. When I was younger, my sister, who is twelve years my senior, had taken on a maternal role in my life, particularly when I was in college living in the East Village and she was in Midtown. She cooked me dinner, we had sleepovers, and she'd hire me to clean her apartment when I was looking for extra money. She was the one I called when I was sick. She was a constant and predictable force in my life, and I loved her for it. I still love her for it. While we saw each other during family gatherings, the bulk of our relationship existed outside of our other relatives. We spent a lot of time alone together, and it felt special. I made a point of visiting her as regularly as I could once she moved to Florida to get the attention I craved from her. There were more occasions when we butted heads as I became a more fully formed adult with opinions that differed from hers; however, we maintained our close bond until our dad got very sick.

Our relationship changed for reasons not relevant to this story and culminated in us not speaking for several years after my dad died. I did not have her to lean on when I was grappling with getting divorced and with the giant reset button I was stomping on. I did not fault her for it then, and I do not fault her for it now, though it hurt and expanded the ever-growing black hole of emptiness that consumed me then. She was gone, my dad was gone, Sam was gone, my friends were gone—and I had never felt so alone.

My life began again in a two-bedroom apartment that felt like clean air but did not feel like home. I had not lived by myself in many years, and doing it over in my late thirties did not carry the same empowering energy it did when I was in my early twenties. I was single, childless, fatherless, dogless, and sisterless, while my remaining friends were growing their families and focusing on their kids. I recall my first trip home from the supermarket after the move. It was a Friday night, and I cried at the bottom of the carpeted one-floor walk up to my door, surrounded by bags I had to lug upstairs myself. Everything about that grocery shopping outing felt so foreign. I no longer had a partner to accompany me and share in the food decision-making. There was nobody around to prepare said purchased foods on nights I had to work late. I was a single bird flying in a sky of flocks. I wasn't sure if I could do it, but I persevered because I did not see any other options.

I spent my early months in my new apartment crying to myself and peeking at the black plastic container full of my dad's ashes that I kept in a small cooler bag in my closet. I leaned into my work and spent my free time eating tater tots or pizza on my couch. I rewatched television shows and movies I had watched with my dad, desperate to hold on to my connection with him, desperate to find a sign from the universe that he thought I was making the right choice by starting over. I was not interested in the outside world.

A friend of mine, unhappy in her own marriage, asked wistfully if I was dating a lot and was shocked to hear that I was not. She told me she would be sleeping with everyone if she were in my position. I never cared about emotionless sex or passing time with people I wasn't interested in. Dating never crossed my mind. Instead, I sat in my grief, even while trying to figure out who I was and what I wanted. It was the first time in a very long time, maybe ever, that I was forced to prioritize myself. I tried to avoid self-destruction by reading books, going to the gym, running, and reconnecting with the close friends and family members I still had.

Adjusting to single life was a challenge, but eventually things felt easier. I looked forward to my nights alone, to not having to compromise or mute my feelings for the sake of someone else's. My apartment started feeling like home. I decorated the walls with photographs I had taken that reminded me life was beautiful and that I was capable of finding beauty no matter how challenging things might feel. By February, I turned my attention to planning a vacation with Camilla and Lia. I would meet them for a week in Paris, where they were stopping off on a longer trip to Israel. I started looking up restaurants and tourist attractions and was reminded how much I love traveling to new places and how trips felt like the most gratifying puzzles to complete.

I found myself sitting alone in an airport at the end of March, awaiting my flight to Paris, and I learned that I love airports and solo plane trips, along with everything that accompanies them. It felt reminiscent of my time in Grand Central Station during my journeys to see my sick dad, but without all the darkness I carried then. When I arrived in Paris, I navigated the airport by myself and found my way to a cab that brought me to my hotel. It was so freeing to do these things. I had spent months living alone as a result of many decisions both in and out of my control, but traveling by myself felt different. Traveling was a choice I made out of something other than necessity, a practice long covered in cobwebs in my brain.

I met up with Camilla and Lia after getting settled, and we were so happy to see one another. Gathering on vacation felt quite different than it had while my dad was sick and in the months that followed. It felt so good to give ourselves permission to be happy. I did not realize it at the time, but the trip was more than just a vacation. We were reorganizing our family and finding ways to stay together without my dad as the linchpin. We wanted to be in each other's lives and to feel all the joy that came with that decision. I felt more connected to Camilla and Lia than I ever had. I felt loved and accepted into a family unit after being rejected by so many of the ones I had previously known. We laughed as we skipped around the city with whimsy. We made lots of very unimportant decisions about eating and activities without any real pressure. I felt like a version of myself that I had previously known was reanimating and growing even larger.

My family left Paris a day before I did, giving me an uninterrupted block of time to do nothing other than consider myself. I walked around the chilly spring city alone and spent positive, undistracted time with myself. I toured Notre Dame, lighting a candle for my father in the entryway. I felt my dad's energy—ironic, considering that my Jewish agnostic father would not have found himself in a church in his organic state. He was there with me that day, and I could sense him in an indescribable way that made me cry from happiness and sadness at the same time—an occurrence I would have scoffed at prior to losing him. I, a woman of science and logic, did not believe in signs from beyond mortality until they were gifted to me in a famous Parisian house of worship.

I strolled through a farmers market and bought sweet, tender dried plums with oblong pits. I spent time outside in the gardens of the Rodin Museum, basking in the sun beneath the marble-carved men above me. I ate breakfast in a café I happened upon, lunch in my hotel room from a crepe vendor outside, and had a three-course dinner in a quintessentially French restaurant with white subway tiles and small, dimly lit tables with jewel tones. A year earlier, sitting alone in a restaurant for a meal would have felt shameful and rushed. I would have worried that the couples at other tables were judging me and avoided looking at anyone. In Paris, I basked in it. I was becoming confident in both old and new ways. I wanted to embrace every opportunity and stop running from things with the potential to be good.

Paris—and specifically my day alone in a foreign city that felt so comforting—was the first time in years that I felt truly present. I knew I would be okay. It felt good to make decisions for myself and pay attention to my wants and needs. Paris did not erase my sadness, but it helped set me on a course to live a life my father would be proud of.

My father used to tell me to consider what he would think before I did anything—and not to do it if I didn't conclude that he would think it was okay. I rolled my eyes at his guidance during my teenage years and early adulthood. I was irked by it at the time. I thought it was my dad being selfish and not caring about what I needed, instead insisting that what he thought was more important than my own ideas. I didn't see that he was trying to impart on me the missing part of my frontal lobe—the decision-making center of our brains that wouldn't fully develop until my midtwenties. He was trying to tell me to make smart choices—not his choices. But my undeveloped teenage brain couldn't see it. Since his death, I don't take him for granted. Paris helped me see that I want to live a life that honors what he gave me.

ELEVEN

I'm almost okay

I am still a work in progress. It has taken a lot to recalibrate my thinking since my dad died. I have gone from being a person who assumed things would go fine to a shakily drawn stick figure convinced that everything would always go horribly. I worried about everything all the time, particularly illness, freak accidents, and death. I became cautious in my relationships—guarded, fearful of loving someone and risking losing them. I saw myself as an unlucky slave to circumstances with no way out. I used to scoff when someone told me I deserved to be happy. *Deserve.* I'd counter that deserve is a philosophical construct and that nobody deserves anything. You get what you get, and you don't get upset. Thinking I had some intrinsic right to goodness felt naive and uninformed.

I have come to accept that even if nobody deserves anything, I am no less deserving than others. Even if we cannot control our ultimate outcomes, perhaps it is possible to stack the odds in our favor. I try to put kindness into the world in hopes of receiving it in return, without the expectation that I should receive it. I consider my dad and his hypothetical perceptions of my choices, as he had wished for me to do so many years earlier. I try to default to patience and let go of the things that do not serve me. Maybe I am not entitled to happiness, but I can certainly do my part to craft a life in search of it.

The Paris trip was the first step in reminding myself that there was good in the world and that I had permission to access it. The next was Michael, the man who would ultimately become my next husband. I had a hard time believing our relationship was real when we started dating. He'd show up at my apartment in the predawn hours before I was awake and clean the snow off my car on his way to work, or leave a note on my windshield or a bouquet of flowers wedged in my car door handle. We'd go on dates and laugh. We'd sit on my couch and cry together, discussing hard moments from our pasts.

I didn't believe him when he told me he loved me. "No," I'd say. "You don't love me. This isn't real. We are in a bubble." He hated it when I called our relationship a bubble or when I inadvertently pushed him away out of fear. For a long time—too long, if you ask him—I was convinced his kind gestures and words were not sustainable. That at some point the niceties would wear off and I would be left with a relationship wrought with conflicts, insecurities, and too much unsaid.

I was shocked to find myself in an emotionally healthy partnership following my divorce and did my best to ruin it before cautiously settling into normalcy. My subconscious defense mechanism was to keep the good at a distance so it would hurt less when life ripped it away, and I did my best to honor that. I struggled to accept that there was someone out there who consistently wanted to hear what I had to say and actively avoided doing things that upset me—someone who loved me enough to want a true, balanced partnership with custom-built parameters that worked for both of us. I kept waiting for the moment when everything would go wrong and retreated in ways that hurt him to avoid being hurt myself. He did not run from my moments of coldness, seeing them for what they were, instead hunkering down in anticipation of me realizing it too. He waited patiently for me to finally accept that our world was real and would not implode. It took a while, but I eventually got it. I let him carry me, kicking and screaming, into happy.

Once I accepted that our connection was indeed genuine and not part of some grand catfishing scheme, I became fearful of what terrors the world might have in store for us. Surrendering to the idea that good existed did not erase my mindset that good could be taken away. I easily jumped to worst-case scenarios when Michael overslept and did not answer a text. I created mental contingency plans for how long I would wait to hear from him before reaching out to his mother or calling the police.

My personal experiences and work know-how assured me that terrible things lay in wait just around the corner, and I wanted to be prepared. I started taking my phone into the shower with me in case of an emergency. I did not want to miss a call, nor did I want to be prevented from making one if I was the one having a heart attack or being burgled. I began sleeping with a pink-and-white steel softball bat at my bedside, should I have to battle an intruder or break through a window to escape a fire. For quite some time, everything that could go wrong did—and I was not prepared when things started going right again.

Michael and I resumed fertility doctor appointments as life started feeling safe again. My desire to have a child did not dissipate after my divorce, and I grew in my confidence to be a parent in a relationship that felt supportive of me doing so. I would be considered a geriatric pregnancy, as doctors so kindly refer to women over thirty-five, and we did not want to waste time. My love for Michael continued to grow when he took time off work to come to bi- and sometimes triweekly bloodwork appointments at a doctor's office an hour and a half from where we lived.

"You don't need to come to my appointments," I'd say.

"I do, because they are our appointments and I love you," he'd reply.

He stayed by my side when I had to give myself hormone injections in my stomach and asked how he could help. I had no idea partners could interact in such a way—a real team.

While the process of fertility tests, treatments, and monitoring was as physically difficult as it was with Sam, the emotional load felt much lighter with Michael. I couldn't believe how much easier a supportive partnership made a hard situation. I no longer felt badly about myself or ashamed for having needs. The tough days were easier, and the disappointments less crushing.

After about four months, I got pregnant. I was overjoyed, but my excitement was tempered by the personal knowledge I had gained about how pregnancies could go wrong—and a healthy baby was by no means guaranteed. I tried to stay calm and optimistic as much as I could throughout the process of another person growing inside my body and borrowing ravenously from my life force. I had read a study detailing a link between anxiety in pregnancy and children with schizophrenia and reminded myself of the conclusion whenever life stressors arose. My worry about worry kept me calm. Things could always go wrong, but this time, for the most part, they didn't. I was shocked when the pregnancy I worked so hard for ultimately resulted in a baby. I was amazed to have an alert, calm-tempered, well baby at that.

After my son was born, I was still preoccupied with worst-case scenarios in a way probably familiar to families who have faced challenges in pregnancy—and that may seem unreasonable to those who have not. We were cautious about who watched him and who could interact with him, creating strict guidelines around handwashing and health that caused animosity with some family members who viewed the world differently than we did. I took his temperature regularly when he cried. As he slept, I'd study the baby monitor for visual evidence that he was breathing, and when it was undetectable, I'd enter his cool, quiet room to watch his tiny chest rise and fall or place my hand beneath his nose to feel the warm air escape his lungs. "He's fine, babe, just like he was ten minutes ago," Michael assured me, but I needed to check. I knew how easily something could be taken from me, and I did not want to miss any signs.

As my son became more durable, I quelled some of my anxieties about his health and could reason away the feeling that he might spontaneously cease to exist for inexplicable reasons. I couldn't, however, believe my luck when my baby loved me as much as I loved him and did not reject me or prefer other adults. My son was not an emotionally abusive boyfriend or a caretaker from my own childhood who inappropriately joked that they would leave in the middle of the night and never come back. He was my child, and all his love required was that I show up consistently with a smile and a made-up song as I fed him, changed him, or lulled him to sleep. It must sound crazy that I needed to wrap my head around such things. Five years later, there are still moments when I am taken by a love I do not have to fight for, and I am astounded by it—and so grateful for it. He has helped etch in my mind that I am indeed worthy of consistent and unconditional positive regard from others. His reminders come in the form of unprompted leg hugs, bedroom snuggles, or moments when I find a small hand placed on mine as we sit on the couch for family movie night.

I have gained a lot of evidence that things can recalibrate and go right, and I continue to work on accepting what has been my reality for the past five years or so. It is impossible to completely unlearn the bad—I still fight my panic when Michael is ten minutes later than expected coming home or when my son sleeps a little longer in the morning than usual. I remind myself that Michael probably wasn't in a terrible car accident but instead stopped for gas or a bunch of bananas at the supermarket, or that occasionally, for no reason at all, kids need extra sleep. Sometimes I slip into planning what I would do if faced with a worst-case scenario— if everything from my recent history that was gifted to me were suddenly ripped away.

That's the thing with anxiety — if we're rational, the things we agonize over could happen, and it's an easy leap for a worried mind to assume that they will. It's important to find ways to remember that a good outcome is just as likely as a bad one, to remind ourselves of the good in our lives. We need to value the good when we have it because it can easily slip away, and it would be a shame to ignore it when it's there.

TWELVE

Keep me in your pocket

There is no secret way to completely move on from the things that injure us deeply. The arc of my dad's sickness and all the events contained within will continue to be the worst things I have gone through—until the next worst thing. Everything that happens to us becomes part of who we are. I am forever changed by what occurred during that time, in both good and bad ways, though I believe, at this point, mostly good. I found takeaways in the grief, some of which I knew at the time, some that helped me through the messy, uncomfortable periods that followed, and some that came to me in retrospect.

They say our bodies essentially regenerate themselves on a cellular level every seven years. It's been more than seven years since the end of this story—and much longer since its onset. Seven plus years later, the physical parts of me that were present when I lost my dad, lost my first child, and lost what I knew of my life are no longer here. I am regenerated. While much of that is also true emotionally, when I think about what happened, I still grieve. Holidays are much harder now, as they can serve as reminders of who is not here, even while fully appreciating who still is.

Michael and I chose to elope because the thought of having a more traditional wedding without our fathers—his father also died young—did not feel like a happy occasion. I was uncomfortably reminded of what it felt like to feed my father as I spoonfed my infant son for the first time, smiling at him through tears at the complexity of how a single moment could be so wonderful and so tragic at the same time. I still have a visceral reaction to hospitals decorated in mint green or that smell like my dad's hospice.

When I initially thought about writing my story, my instinct was to see how I could put a funny spin on it. That's my jam—trying to find humor in situations in hindsight. I'm usually pretty good at it, but there isn't much humor to be found here. The story of my father getting sick and dying, the story of my miscarriage, the story of a marriage ending—they all felt like an unstoppable, shit-covered snowball rolling down a mountain in slow motion, growing until it reached the bottom and ultimately exploded in a suffocating pile. The story was far from a comedy, and it felt like a disservice to try to make it one. Humor is helpful, but only humor—only tending to the positives—is not. To truly move forward, we need to look hard in its beady, desperate eyes and stand up to it before we can figure out how to reframe it.

So yes, when life felt bleak, I ate pastries, made awkward jokes, and took introspective train rides—and that was peaceful, but that's about it. The skills and strategies I developed, and strongly encourage you to use, did not make things better. At best, they made the sadness bearable and kept me from completely losing my mind, which, at the time, was sufficient. When we are in crisis, our brains go into self-preservation mode. We detach, we minimize—not because we want to, but because fully confronting the situation in real time is both impossible and meaningless.

We can't fully prepare ourselves for how we will feel when we encounter a tragedy—or a heap of tragedies happening at once. But there are pieces of information you can keep in your pocket as you navigate your days and make choices about who you keep close. Here are some steps I recommend taking to prepare for the inevitable. I often thought about my father's perspectives on decisions after he died: how important it is to keep the idea of a reasonable person in mind and bounce our impulses off that schema before acting. I use the frustrating question he asked me as a teenager to guide my adult judgment, framing my decisions and how I choose to treat people. My dad's death made me a softer, more compassionate person for a myriad of reasons that I will share with you, friends, in the form of lessons.

You Need to Ask All Your Questions

Make sure you say whatever you need to say to your loved ones and search for the important answers while you still can. Basically, take the initiative to foster a fulfilling sense of intimacy and connectedness in your relationships. Have the hard conversations before it feels like you must—or before you can't have them anymore. Try to wrap your head around what it truly means to accept that time is not guaranteed and that we do not all get to live long, uncomplicated lives and die peacefully in our sleep, surrounded by loved ones. Let this motivate you, not riddle you with fear. The distinction is important and can be a challenge at times. Knowing that everything I value can disappear at any moment helps keep me intentional in how I communicate with my remaining loved ones.

I missed opportunities to have deep conversations about life and death with my father, joking instead about assisted suicide. When the hypothetical became reality, I sensed that my dad's perspective on the end of his life had changed. Mine certainly had, and I couldn't have done anything to help him along, even if I had wanted to. I don't regret not having that weight permanently grafted to my shoulders. I do regret not hearing more from him or learning more from him. I regret not realizing that his attempts to discuss his Will were his way of talking to me about death. He opened a door that I gently closed in his face because I thought it was polite to do so. I decided it was what he needed. Turns out my dad knew better than I did. I wish I had given him the space to say what he needed to. Let the people you care about tell you what they're looking to tell you, and try to get your important answers.

My fully formed adult brain wishes younger me had the capacity to bring up difficult subjects with my father. What was it like growing up with a mother who ended up hospitalized? Tell me more about my grandparents. Let's talk about that day at the cemetery, or that drive to Brooklyn, or your life in Brooklyn. My dad and I rarely commiserated about serious shared events as they occurred, let alone discussed the things that shaped his past. If I had known my time with him was so limited, chances are I would have been bolder. Learning more about him and getting some answers to questions I had about my early life would have seemed more important. I assumed the day would come when we would have that talk—where we'd sit on a bench overlooking Jones Beach and discuss hard things without making eye contact while gazing out at the ocean.

My fantasy of having that intimate conversation never came to fruition because my dad's life did not take the course I expected. Time is not infinite, nor is it guaranteed. Chances are there will be a tomorrow for most of us—but who knows? Figure out the crucial things about the people in your life and ask your questions before your opportunity to do so is taken away.

I do regret not having all the important conversations with my dad. Instead of letting helpless frustration ignite a fuse that leads to endless self-loathing, I carry that regret into my current relationships in hopes of not making the same mistake again. If the important people in your life were to vanish, what would you wish you had said to them? What would you wish you knew about them? Take the opportunity to give and get the information that will leave you too fulfilled to have much room for regret later on.

You Can Understand Things from Another Person's Perspective Without Making Assumptions

There are many anecdotes that felt one way when they were happening but have taken on a wholly different meaning now that I have gained more perspective. I'll share a couple of more poignant ones. My dad often talked about positivity—relentless positivity, as he called it—and would not entertain conversations he thought were negative. He spoke about beating his cancer, about getting better, about making it to Lia's college graduation. He assured everyone that somehow he knew he would not die until he was in his nineties. At the time, we thought he was in denial, delusional, or maybe it was a result of his brain being broken. How could he honestly think and say such things that were so obviously untrue? He was sick with something incurable that medication was pausing but not stopping, and like a small stick jammed in a door to prop it open, one day someone would push hard enough, snapping the twig and slamming the door shut.

I look at my dad's choices differently now and realize that he probably didn't fully believe what he was saying. My dad was a positive person. He spent a lot of time—both in health and sickness—focusing on making sure the rest of us were okay. But he was also probably scared of what he logically knew to be true about his situation. He was likely not ready to accept that he had a terminal illness and would die long before he was prepared for his time to be up. I spent so much time managing my reaction to his sickness that I nearly forgot to consider he was a living person to whom this was happening.

The difference between my dad's views on life and mine also manifested in our attitudes toward high-fat foods. My dad, as you may recall, was very concerned about doing anything that might raise his cholesterol, and as such, he refused to eat cheese. He picked it off things, ate around it, and was generally averse to its existence. For a while, he allowed himself to indulge in soy-based cheese, but when the cancer began, the manufactured "dairy" stopped as well. When I cooked for him, he would ask me to make chicken Parmesan without cheese. I, who did not share his aversion, piled the cheese on mine, and he would eat around the smallest shred that unintentionally transferred from my side of the baking dish to his.

I challenged his approach to cheese because I didn't understand it. "Live it up," I'd say. "Now is the time to eat the cheese, and the steak, and the French fries you love so much."

I'd try to plan trips to Nathan's for beloved hot dogs and crinkle-cut French fries—all things my dad had once cherished and had since forsaken in the name of healthy living. Logically, he didn't need to be healthy anymore, which I viewed as the one advantage of a death sentence. He'd wave off my comments and ignore my food fantasies. I thought it was ridiculous—a waste of the best excuse for indulgence. A last, decadent hoorah that he was letting pass him by. I didn't see that he wasn't eating the cheese because he was terrified of what eating the cheese meant. He wasn't ready to accept that there would be few subsequent hoorahs.

In keeping with his persistence, my father maintained his unwavering diet until the end. At the time, I was focused on the topical and failed to see the deeper meaning behind his behavior. I tried to impose my perspective without honoring his own. I get it now. Sometimes the things we say and do aren't so clear-cut. As caregivers and supporters, we bear some responsibility for looking beneath the surface. In quiet moments, take a step back from difficult situations and search for empathy. Try to imagine what it must be like to be the one actually facing the tragedy, and consider your loved ones from their perspective. It may help you understand them better—and give you insight into why a decision that seems ludicrous or inconsequential to you might be deeply important to them.

While we strive to develop empathy, it's important to stop the pendulum from swinging too far in the opposite direction. Do not assume you know what others are thinking; such assumptions can lead to misguided decisions. It's a natural reflex to pull away from someone else's pain because of our own discomfort. We think about how we don't know what to say or do, and so we choose to do nothing—to give the person space. We assume they'll reach out when they're ready, so we sit uncomfortably on the sidelines.

When I had my miscarriage, when my dad died, and when I got divorced, I stopped hearing from some of the people who had been close to me. They assumed I wanted distance and privacy, when what I really needed was to be supported and seen—something to make me feel less like an outcast from society. I certainly didn't want to discuss the hard details of what I was going through on repeat, but it would have been nice to hear about someone else's regular day or see a funny picture.

Reach out to the people in your life unapologetically when they're struggling, and let them decide what comes next. Try to do so unselfishly, without personalizing the response you get. If there's no text or call back, it's probably more about them than about you—and may have no bearing on how they feel about hearing from you.

There were many texts I received during the hardest times that I didn't respond to because my hands felt as if they were made of lead and my brain was bogged down with tar. Still, hearing from people made me feel slightly better. Once I was able to gather my thoughts and find my words, I let those people know how appreciated they were. I got my share of intrusive or poorly timed questions that I certainly didn't enjoy, but just knowing there was a world out there waiting for me when I was ready made me feel good. When there's nothing to say, say anything.

Live Each Day with an Awareness That There Is Always the Potential for Regret

We all have the capacity to say cruel things or to not return a phone call on principle—over one thing or another—with the subconscious assumption that the stakes aren't that high or that there's always time. But what would it be like to assume there isn't always time? To act in a way that makes sense in a world where there may be no opportunities for do-overs?

I began approaching many decisions from a productive fatalist perspective when my father was dying, hoping to find a way to ensure I'd be as comfortable with my choices as possible. I knew that at some point my dad would be gone, and that I—and my own judgment of myself—would be what remained in his wake. I wanted to feel good about who I was and how I showed up when there would be no chance for a second take. While there are certainly some things I could focus on if I wanted to feel regret, for the most part, I can face myself each day knowing I did the best I could—and all that I could—during a difficult time, one that came without an instruction manual.

I carry this attitude with me still, fully aware that every relationship has an unknown ending. It might seem dramatic to regularly toss out the hypothetical of never seeing someone again unexpectedly, but I don't think it is. I don't think I'm melodramatic—though by this point, maybe you disagree.

I quietly ask myself, usually in an inner voice reminiscent of my dad's cool, even tone, "Is this how you want to end things? Is this how you want someone to remember you? Is this really the last thing you want to say?" Then I try to adjust my behavior as needed.

It's not always easy, and sometimes I fail. It's easy to respond to hurt with hurt or annoyance with annoyance, but I don't want to. I don't want to be the person who gets in one last dig during an argument or who doesn't call someone because they think that person should be calling them. I use my dad's untimely death to help give me perspective on what matters. I am finally doing what he asked of me—considering him in my decision-making. I know he is proud.

A crucial part of living a life with minimal regrets is not punishing ourselves for past situations we cannot change. It doesn't serve us to look back on events already etched in marble and try to imagine how they could have been different. In cognitive behavioral therapy, we encourage our clients to avoid using "should" because it implies judgment. When we say, "I should have done this," we're indicting our past selves with our current knowledge. We take our current perspective and hold our past perspective responsible for it.

It's helpful to seek forgiveness from ourselves when reflecting on unchangeable events. We don't know what we don't know, and often we don't realize what we don't know until we begin to orbit outside a situation rather than exist within it. It is okay to reflect. In fact, a huge part of growth involves owning the parts of ourselves we don't like—and then doing something about them so our futures can feel different.

Denying Your Emotions Does Not Solve Problems

I generally kept my feelings to myself throughout my dad's illness. It seemed selfish to do otherwise—to make someone else's suffering about my own. I thought my internal experience was less valid than my father's, convinced I didn't have as much right to be upset, and I shoved my thoughts deep into the place in my abdomen where stomach aches and sleepless nights manifest. I assumed I was doing the right thing. I assumed I was being strong for my family by putting on a reassuring face that everything would be okay.

I was particularly cognizant of my emotions in front of Lia. I recalled from my childhood that seeing adults cry was disarming, and I didn't want to be some emotionally dysregulated and unpredictable force in her life. When I saw her, we giggled and skipped down the street. I pretended to struggle when she took hundreds of rapid-fire selfies on my phone after stealthily plucking it from my pocket—or unstealthily grabbing it from my hands. We didn't talk about our dad being sick or what it was like for her to live with someone who had changed into a new, worse person after her sleepaway camp summer. I wanted to give her some space to be a typical kid who did silly kid things.

While having the chance to take a break from all the sadness was probably helpful for her, the flip side—the extreme pretense that nothing was wrong—was not. I have come to understand that I was not, in fact, modeling healthy strength for Lia. I was teaching her that feelings are unacceptable and that it's not okay to be sad when sad things happen. My emotions felt scary, and I unintentionally conveyed to her that hers were, too.

Healthy coping with grief requires balance. Though it would have been equally unacceptable to be constantly hysterical, talking a little about feelings would have helped Lia understand the situation we were in. It also would have helped set her up to be an emotionally available person—a quality closely related to gratifying adult relationships. Positive modeling is important, arguably just as important as genetics in determining who we become and how we engage with the world around us.

Sometimes we would profess, "We are Landesses! We are strong!"—and we are. Lia is one of the strongest people I know, having endured so much more than most can imagine. I am strong, too—now much more than when I was younger. I used to think my strength came from being stone-faced amidst chaos, but having and expressing emotions in a healthy way is what makes us strong.

Embracing my vulnerabilities, rather than fearfully running from them.

It's important to learn how to shamelessly own your feelings and surround yourself with people who make it safe to do so. Cry when something is sad, even if you happen to be feeling sad at a bus stop or in a coffee shop.

Successfully moving forward requires dealing with your feelings about what is in front of you—not just stuffing them down or moving them aside for the sake of some false assumption about strength. You'll be doing yourself—and those around you who could use some teaching—a great service.

Every Day Is a Gift

I know—saying "every day is a gift" sounds basic, like something that should be printed above a framed picture of a kitten or stitched on a needlepoint pillow. I get it. Previous versions of myself would have rolled their eyes at me for saying something so seemingly unprofound.

Sometimes I'm embarrassed to share this tidbit with others, fearing the optics—that it sounds like I'm minimizing people's pain and trying to package it in a big-box-store brand of psychology they have no interest in purchasing. I'm not doing that. Promise. I certainly did not feel like life was a gift during my dad's illness or amid my personal struggles related to my miscarriage. I don't think this is the kind of advice that will be overwhelmingly well received in the midst of a catastrophe. I certainly wouldn't have wanted someone to tell me how great the world was the day my dad was diagnosed—or the day he died.

Having an understanding that every day is something we are gifted—by some magical combination of science, circumstance, luck, and religion—helps soften the edges of jagged times. Believing that every day is a gift is not the same as the false presumption that every day is wonderful. Every day isn't wonderful, but every day we have is something given to us that not everybody receives.

This understanding is not meant to negate the bad or to convince ourselves that things are good when they don't feel good. Things can be both bad and good at the same time. Reminding ourselves that we are fortunate to be alive—to see the sun rise or set, to eat something we enjoy, to smile at a pet we love, to laugh on the phone—is something our lost loved ones no longer have. If we are here, we have the chance to feel better and to do something about our circumstances. We can create our own space for hope by reminding ourselves that we are fortunate for what we do have. Moderate positivity.

It takes work, but we can retrain our brains to focus on the positive. Once, in high school, I was chatting with a friend as we walked through a park to meet a larger group. I told him I was tired, that it was hot. Maybe I mentioned being thirsty or hungry or needing to pee. Eventually, he looked at me and said, "You complain a lot." My instinct was to correct him. I wasn't complaining; I was just talking—making observations about the world and my place in it as we waded into a small patch of nature in Queens.

His comment stuck with me, and I spent the evening apart from our group in self-reflection as everyone else drank keg beer from red plastic cups and listened to punk rock mixtapes on a boombox. Was I a complainer? I didn't feel like a particularly negative person, nor did I see my statements as complaining. But I realized that making negatively skewed comments does come across as complaining. I could just as easily have said that I was happy to be out or excited to see our friends on a nice summer evening. I could have told him that I was glad he met up with me and was walking with me. I felt all those nice things at the time—they just didn't seem like the kinds of things people discussed.

In the years since, I've realized that I had been socialized to have negatively skewed conversations based on how some of the adults around me communicated. Some people use self-expression to focus on what is wrong, while others do the opposite. After that night in the woods, I began paying attention to my speaking instincts. I started holding back the negative thoughts that could be perceived as complaining, instead choosing to focus on what was going right—or to say nothing if it didn't seem like anything was going right. I encourage you to pay attention to your communication style and note whether your tendency is to fixate on problems—and challenge yourself to do something about it. Match each complaint with a positive counterpoint, and withhold negative comments that don't hold productive value.

Everyone stranded on the side of the road with a flat tire thinks some explicit version of "This is bullshit," but the only one worth listening to is the person who knows how to use the jack. If we actively choose to change how we communicate, we alter how we see the world, and it becomes easier to accept that every day is a gift. Maybe we learn to appreciate that we know how to change the tire more than we're upset about needing to change it at all. Or maybe an eagle flies overhead as we're changing the tire, and we realize we wouldn't have seen it if the universe hadn't forced us to stop.

If You Seek Out Gratitude, You Can Find It

One of the harder—but more useful—ways to manage grief is to search for the good in ugly situations. Gratitude takes work and was not something I could find much of while my dad was sick or afterward. While I appreciated the opportunity to have a train ride and a pastry as part of my dad's doctor visits, I certainly was not grateful that he had gotten sick so I could have those opportunities. There would have been much easier ways to justify eating a croissant once a month.

In the years since, I have recognized that I am grateful for my bonds with Lia and Camilla, which came about through the unfortunate circumstances we were forced to face. Our relationship has flourished following my dad's illness, and its strength is very much a byproduct of what we went through.

Hard as it is for even me to believe, I am also grateful for the miscarriage that ravaged me physically and emotionally and played a role in destroying my first marriage. I am not glad to have lost a baby or to have been placed in a situation where I feared bleeding to death. I am certainly not glad to have been responsible for dangling a small, shiny object just beyond my dad's grasp and then ripping it away before he could grab it in the last months of his life. Without the miscarriage, there would have been different consequences—ones that could not have been undone. I likely would not have been able to spend as much time as I did with my dad had I remained pregnant, particularly while he was in hospice, a place brimming with terminal illness. If I had been pregnant, I would have had to tend more to my well-being; but once I was not, I could stay focused on him. I remind myself how fortunate I am to have spent as much time with my father as I did, which brings me peace during the hard moments that continue to arise. It's definitely not a "Thank God for that miscarriage!" warm-and-fuzzy feeling, but I can appreciate how one squeaky door closing forced open another—one I was glad to have the chance to walk through.

Everything that happens to us and around us shapes who we are, and I like who I am now. I am bolder, more confident, and better able to appreciate what I have to offer myself and others. I realize I did not care much for the person I was before all the tragedy. I was timid, insecure, and self-loathing—not the most appealing of qualities. I am grateful that I found a way to grow. All the loss contributed to the kind of person I am—the kind of wife and daughter I am, and the kind of mother I am. Hard times highlight how important our decisions are, and my dad and my fertility hurdles have made me more intentional. I'm not sure I would have figured it out without all that darkness.

There Is Something Good Every Day, Even on the Hardest Days

Something good happens every day. Maybe it sounds corny, naïve, or untrue, but it isn't. If we prime ourselves to focus on the positive, we can find it. To be clear, I'm not saying something great happens every day—something great does not happen every day, and the good things that do happen do not always outweigh the bad. I think of the bright sun on the day my dad died, its rays warming my skin as I walked to my car to drive to him for the last time. Remembering the sun in that moment is a small positive amid a whirlwind of negatives, but appreciating the sun does not outweigh my dad's death nor my intimate knowledge of what his death was like. Still, it was something.

My journey into what I call moderate positivity began in a professional capacity long before my father's passing. One of my responsibilities at work was to run a community meeting with the patients under my care. By design, the community meeting was a weekly gathering for clinicians, direct care staff, and patients to communicate about what was happening on the floor and to address any concerns related to unit or hospital functioning. In reality, the community meeting was a time no one looked forward to—clinicians entering patient living spaces and direct care working spaces in an inconvenient way. Patients yelled at staff, at one another, and complained about clogged toilets and burnt-out lightbulbs. Sometimes the meeting ended abruptly when a serious argument erupted. On one occasion, the meeting had to be stopped after a patient punched the man sitting next to him, breaking his jaw. The *crack* of the jaw shattering still echoes in my head. At best, the meetings were unpleasant; at worst, hospital activity was shut down as we waited for an ambulance to enter the compound.

When I started running my own unit, I wanted the meetings to be different, to be a space that did not make people feel worse about their situation and did not result in broken bones. I created a structure for the meetings to curtail the angry freeform ranting, and entitled the last section *Positive Notes*. I asked my thirty captive and begrudging listeners to tell me something good during my first meeting, and the room fell silent. I waited for a spontaneous response, and when one did not come, I told the patients that I would remain in the dayroom, essentially their living room, until someone told me something good that happened or that they were looking forward to. They viewed my request as juvenile and as demeaning to the very real situations that brought them to the hospital and that they faced daily while there. I countered that people can't get better if they spend all their time exclusively thinking about and talking about the worst parts of their lives and held firm with my request. Eventually, one man raised his hand and shared that he was expecting a package. I thanked him, and the meeting was adjourned.

I made my demand weekly at the end of each meeting, and slowly more people started sharing small joys: the opportunity to speak to a loved one on the phone, excitement over a party, a good lunch in the cafeteria. Over time, the patients began sharing things they were proud of and openly complimented one another for kind acts during the week. They would applaud when someone said something vulnerable. For those brief moments, they became supportive of one another and slightly let their guards down..

The connectedness we were creating began to manifest outside the meetings—there were fewer fights on the unit and fewer instances of patients screaming demands at staff. Thinking about the good helped them focus less on the bad. Talking about Taco Tuesday didn't negate the reasons they were in the hospital or how difficult their futures might be, but it made the hard stuff more bearable. If we prime ourselves to search for good, we can find it— and doing so is what helps us through the hard times.

Camilla arranged a memorial ceremony for my father a week after his death in lieu of a proper funeral—something we knew he would not have wanted. The memorial was hard. It marked the first time I returned to his apartment building since he entered hospice, and I was tasked with giving the main eulogy—a difficult feat, especially since I had to get through it without completely losing it in front of a room full of people. While crying is okay, it felt important for me to say what I had to say about my dad and to be heard by our loved ones.

When I recall that day, I easily recall how heavy his loss weighed on me. If I wanted to torture myself, I could focus on how, in a receiving line at the ceremony's conclusion, the wife of one of his closest friends congratulated me on having a baby. I can focus on how the reminder of being pregnant—and then not—at my father's memorial shot through my abdomen like a fiery arrow, or the look of horror on her face when she realized she had inadvertently said something terrible. I can think about how my dad probably had a happy phone call with his friend announcing my pregnancy, and how the message of the miscarriage never made it to his friend's wife amidst all he was going through. I can think of those things and feel awful about myself, or I can decide to shift my focus elsewhere.

When I think of my father's ceremony, I choose to remember the brief moments of laughter I shared with Lia and Camilla as the ceremony began. Randomly, several millipedes were crawling on the floor of the Upper West Side meeting room. "Don't step on them," Camilla warned Lia in a whispered, urgent voice. "They're Dad." She was convinced that my father was coming to us in bug form when we needed his energy most, which made Lia and me laugh. I laughed briefly before enduring the most difficult public speaking experience I have had. I choose to think of a comforting nap taken in the arms of someone who used to love me following the ceremony, as the sun warmed us through large windows facing the Hudson. Those small, contented moments bring me a sense of peace, while all the other memories make me anxious and sad—feelings I no longer want to hold. I focus on how cozy my friends' hugs felt that morning, and how the smiles glowing in their eyes were full of support. None of that head-tilt pity.

I often share the community meeting story with my patients in therapy to illustrate that if men who had committed serious crimes due to psychiatric symptoms—and who would likely spend large parts of their lives in a prison hospital—could find something good about their day, then anyone can. I share that same perspective here. If those men could find something good, if I could find something good in my father's death, you can too. Try it. What is it like, during stressful or non-stressful times, to end each day thinking of one thing that went right and one thing to look forward to tomorrow?

You Deserve Something for Yourself

When things are hard, make sure you give yourself something to look forward to. Having a positive focus, no matter how small, can give you hope that good still exists and that some form of joy is coming. I surely would not have been disappointed if I hadn't had a sad reason to travel to Manhattan to have a hospital bedside lunch with my father, but I tried to view those lunches as an opportunity I wouldn't otherwise have had. I would tell myself, *I have to go into Manhattan to do something hard and sad, and I have earned a cheeseburger.*

I applied a similar strategy in my daily life before my dad's illness, too.

When I was younger, frozen boxed mac and cheese was one of my favorite foods. It was the meal I chose for myself for dinner if my parents went out together and left me home with a babysitter. It became my comfort meal in college on nights I decided to stay in instead of going out drinking with friends in uncomfortable shoes. That frozen boxed mac and cheese is as terrible for you as it is delicious—loaded with fat, sodium, and preservatives, cooked in the microwave in a black plastic container. I retrospectively gasp at the toll that mac and cheese must have taken on my unsuspecting internal organs. At some point, it moved from my regular rotation to something saved for sad special occasions—my "self-pity dinner," as I called it. When I got broken up with, did poorly on a test, or got sick, I'd remind myself that I could at least have the mac and cheese. There was something comforting in giving myself permission to do something that was not good for me but was for me.

I am not advocating for you to load your body with carbs, chemicals, and fat to feel better, or that you rely on emotional eating as a long-term coping mechanism. I am proposing that you find your own mac and cheese—something you give yourself or do for yourself during hard times when it can be difficult to conjure something to look forward to. Your mac and cheese could be a massage, a walk, or a guilty-pleasure television show.

While I occasionally indulged in my literal mac and cheese, more often I relied on the metaphorical ones: self-care rituals like hair appointments and manicures that allowed me to connect with others casually and talk about something other than cancer and struggles. Self-care made my hard routine a little more bearable. I imagined my yoga class creating invisible body armor that I wore until it was time for the next session. I sought out things that made me feel strong. I made playlists of empowering music and fought the urge to sink into the saddest soundtracks imaginable—the ones I was naturally drawn to. I created opportunities to feel good about myself at a time when the universe was not readily providing them.

Its easy to forget ourselves when we are overtaken by our emotions. I encourage you to find the small ways to fight through and remember who you are whenever possible. Taking care of yourself in the midst of the hard is not selfish and makes the eventual return to normalcy easier.

Grief Never Ends, and Things Will Never Go Back to Normal

As my father was dying, I sought some relief in thinking that, at some point, I would feel okay again—would feel like my old self. I made assumptions based on something I did not know, because wouldn't it be nice to one day just be fine?

I am reminded often that I knew nothing about death and grief before I was neck-deep in it. The process of losing my dad to GBM will never disappear from the essence of who I am; it has become a core part of me and has shaped both my history and my future. I can't go back to being the person I was before he was gone, and though I wish every day that he were here to see who I have become—as a psychologist, a parent, and a human—I do not want to go back to the way things were before. I do not want to be eternally and continually sad about my dad, but I do appreciate that there are times when I do feel sad and am reminded of our connection. There are times when I think of him, instances when I feel him with me, and I cry in those moments. My son is well acquainted with my sadness—his five-year-old hands often wiping tears from my face when he notices and asks if I am thinking about his grandpa, whom he never met but knows so much about.

I'll point out that there is a difference between being changed by something and being destroyed by it. Four or five months after my miscarriage, during a conversation about my continued sadness, Sam told me, "You can't be eternally ruined by something." I think he thought he was being helpful, but the angry diatribe he received in response from me quickly convinced him otherwise. Ruined. Though I felt broken—no, pulverized—I wasn't ruined then, and I am not ruined now. I navigated my grief and ultimately moved forward in a way that feels almost okay.

If we find lessons in the bad things that happen to us, we grow. If we use those bad things as excuses to rationalize destructive or unhealthy behavior, we get worse. I have chosen to grow. I forgive those who did not behave well when my dad was sick and when I was battling pregnancy loss. I do not hold on to the kind of resentment or anger that seeped from my dad when the tumor in his brain attacked the thick walls he had built around the memories that harmed him.

At times, there is a fine line between wellness and self-destruction in the face of grief. Even as I write this, I'm settled into a place that feels both bad and good at the same time. I feel myself hunched over in a small black box twenty feet underground, and that sadness is familiar and comforting in some ways. But I know the consequences of staying in that little box, and I know that's not how I want to live my life.

Gwenn and I have come back together post-everything. Our relationship feels like a warm blanket, yet it also does not feel the same. The distance between us taught me about both of us. What I learned is that I don't get to dictate who people are or how they show up—they get to choose. All I can do is decide whether to accept their terms or not. I recognize Gwenn's terms, and I know what our relationship is and isn't. I choose to accept what is because I've lived through the alternative, and that felt worse than what we have.

In my new worldview, there is a balance between sadness and good times. I can feel fulfilled while knowing that I will never get back what I lost. I can feel good despite knowing that whatever new and exciting puzzle pieces I craft will never fit perfectly into old spaces. Realizing that things would never return to what I thought normal was probably wouldn't have helped me understand what came next, but it may have helped me sit in my reality and fully appreciate my last encounters with my dad rather than wishing for the hard part to be over in anticipation of something that would never come.

Try to find ways to calibrate your expectations so that when the hard times ultimately pass, you can appreciate what you have and are not left grappling with disappointment.

You Have the Power to Recreate Your Narrative

What story do you tell yourself about how the people in your life support you?

Make sure the individuals you lean on are capable of meeting your expectations—and if they aren't, find those who are. Creating a support network may require you to reconfigure your definition of family. Those biologically or legally bound to us do not possess a unique capacity to meet our needs. There is nothing embedded in our DNA that guarantees support. Countless families experience discord due to loss, and it is often shocking to see a darker, wounded, or less capable side of the people who once helped us celebrate our birthdays as children. I don't mean to sound hopeless. I am not saying everyone is destined to be disappointed, but disappointment is always a possibility—especially if we are not vigilant about it.

Make sure your friends and family show up, support you, and validate you. Who is there for the good times—and who is there when things get hard? How do the people in your life handle minor conflicts and stressors? How we deal with the small hiccups is usually a good indication of how we will handle the big ones. We can use minor disagreements or times of need as rehearsals for the main event. Will your loved ones hear your needs when you're upset that they didn't bring you soup when you had a cold—and then show you something different next time? If so, those are your people. If not, it may be time to reassess their value.

I had a lot of grief reactions reflected back at me between my miscarriage, my dad's death, and my divorce. A lot of sideways pity head tilts when I shared my news. The head tilts were accompanied by emotional math when I spoke about my dad. "How old was he?" they asked. When I said he died at sixty-nine, some people uttered "oh, okay" and nodded their heads with relief in their voices—as if they had decided sixty-nine was old and therefore an acceptable age to die, ignoring that he had been sick for about five years and that those five years were torture for everyone. Forgetting that the death of a loved one is always challenging, no matter the person's age. Sixty-nine made sense to them and was somehow less tragic than someone dying younger. I'm not quite sure what the formula is or at what age a person's death shifts from something that does not make sense to something that does. In reality, one does not exist.

To those of you grieving, find supporters who aren't so blatantly self-referential—who don't try to console themselves by comparing your losses to their own prospects. To those of you engaging with loved ones struggling in grief, stop cocking your head to the side and making the pursed-lip, frowny faces straight out of children's drawings in response to hard news. Find other ways to be supportive that will actually feel like empathy.

Plenty of healthy support exists, and it may come from unexpected sources. I assumed Sam would be the one to console me. He wasn't, and I should have seen it coming. I did not expect my dad's third wife to be one of the people who tethered me to sanity and hope during my hardest times. If I had closed myself off to the idea of her, I would have missed an important opportunity to connect and build my own version of family. We are family because we chose to be, despite all odds. Our relationship has evolved beyond our shared grief over the loss of my dad, her husband. We have been there for one another through so much good since then: the birth of my son, Lia's milestones, and her journey into happiness with a new partner. As I write this, I am sitting on a balcony at a Cancun resort, watching the sunrise and preparing to officiate her wedding. We created the kind of sustainable connection my dad wanted for us. I know he is so proud.

ACKNOWLEDGMENTS

Human beings do not do anything alone, and this book is no exception.

None of this would have been possible without the mass of people in my corner, holding my hand and cheering me on. I'd like to thank my writing coach, Ali Tugwell, and the team at selfpublishing.com for giving me the structure I needed to get writing, and for holding me accountable. Thanks to my editor, Katelynn Koonz, and her team for doing their best to help me find and organize my voice into coherent sentences, and to TJ Marquis and Dakota Jackson for making my book cover dreams come true. Thank you to the real Lia and Camilla for their unwavering love and support, and to my mom Alice for being my number one fan. I'd like to thank the friends and family that stuck with me through my journey, as well the ones who didn't. There are lessons everywhere, and sometimes the gifts we received but did not want are just as valuable as the ones we have asked for. Finally, I would like to thank my husband Michael and my son for their unconditional love and for showing me every day that good lurks around even the darkest corners. You are my fuel, and I am forever grateful for you.

ABOUT THE AUTHOR

Amanda Landes earned her Psy.D. in school/community psychology and has been helping people carve their own paths for nearly two decades in both inpatient and outpatient settings. She has written for school publications and served as an NYU film critic and a quarterly publication editor. She has coauthored a textbook chapter and published an award-winning dissertation on a rehabilitation program for juvenile delinquents. Her current work focuses on balancing her professional experience as a psychologist while sharing her "humanness" and the issues we all face.

Amanda recently relocated from New York to Florida. When she is not working, seeing clients in her private practice, or conducting forensic evaluations, she enjoys spending time with her husband, son, and two Great Danes.

URGENT PLEA!

Thank You For Reading My Book!

I truly appreciate all of your feedback and
love hearing what you have to say.

I need your input to help make the next version of this
book better, as well as to improve my future books.

Please take two minutes now to leave a
helpful review on Amazon and let me
know what you thought of the book.

Thanks so much!

Amanda

www.ingramcontent.com/pod-product-compliance
Lightning Source LLC
Chambersburg PA
CBHW020247130626
46549CB00005B/2111